符号中国 SIGNS OF CHINA

金银器

GOLD AND SILVER ARTICLES

"符号中国"编写组 ◎ 编著

中央民族大学出版社
China Minzu University Press

图书在版编目(CIP)数据

金银器：汉文、英文 /"符号中国"编写组编著. —北京：中央民族大学出版社，2024.3
（符号中国）
ISBN 978-7-5660-2328-5

Ⅰ.①金… Ⅱ.①符… Ⅲ.①金银器（考古）—介绍—中国—汉、英 Ⅳ.①K876.43

中国国家版本馆CIP数据核字（2023）第257179号

符号中国：金银器 GOLD AND SILVER ARTICLES

编　　著	"符号中国"编写组
策划编辑	沙　平
责任编辑	周雅丽
英文指导	李瑞清
英文编辑	邱　械
美术编辑	曹　娜　郑亚超　洪　涛
出版发行	中央民族大学出版社
	北京市海淀区中关村南大街27号　　邮编：100081
	电话：（010）68472815（发行部）　传真：（010）68933757（发行部）
	（010）68932218（总编室）　　　　（010）68932447（办公室）
经 销 者	全国各地新华书店
印 刷 厂	北京兴星伟业印刷有限公司
开　　本	787 mm×1092 mm　1/16　印张：9.5
字　　数	123千字
版　　次	2024年3月第1版　2024年3月第1次印刷
书　　号	ISBN 978-7-5660-2328-5
定　　价	58.00元

版权所有　侵权必究

"符号中国"丛书编委会

唐兰东　巴哈提　杨国华　孟靖朝　赵秀琴

本册编写者

胥　敏

前言 Preface

黄金拥有天然艳丽的色彩和炫目耀眼的光泽，白银则以洁白纯亮的色泽受世人喜爱，它们是金属中自然天生的贵族。用金银打造的器具，是大自然的创造与人类智慧的完美结合，拥有灿烂炫目的色彩和千年不变的高贵品质。高贵的金银器不仅美化了人们的生活，还影响了人类的思想；不仅代表了财富，还是身份地位和富贵等级的标志。

中国古代金银工艺历史悠久，金银器制作的重点始终是其审美价值。即便是实用性，也是巧妙地隐藏于审美价值之中，从而使人们在欣赏金银器

The gold possesses natural gorgeous color and glaring luster when the silver is beloved for its spotlessly white tincture, both which are the born nobles in metals. Utensils forged in gold or silver ideally combine the work of nature and human intelligence, and has the brilliant color and perdurable high-class quality. The noble gold and silver articles not only embellished our life, but also impacted the way we think. Furthermore they are also the symbol of social status, riches and honor.

China has a long history of gold and silver handicraft. The aesthetic value is the most important in the forging of gold and silver articles, even the practicability remains skillfully

的形象、色泽的同时，满足现实需要。现在，就让我们步入金碧辉煌、银光闪耀的世界，阅读那多彩的金银器画图，感受中国深厚的金银文化。

under the cover of the aesthetic value, so that people can meet the real life when appreciating the beauty. Now, let's step into this magnificent world, learn the colorful history, and experience the profound gold and silver culture of China.

目 录 Contents

中国金银器概述
Overview of China's Gold and Silver Articles 001
源远流长的金银文化
Long History of Gold and Silver Culture 002

历代金银器的特点
Characteristics of the Gold and Silver
Articles in Different Dynasties 008

金银器的工艺
The Craft of the Gold and Silver Articles 043
锻造技术
Forging Technology 044

装饰工艺
Decoration Craft 058

纹饰工艺
Pattern Craft 080

金银器的器形
The Shape of the Gold and Silver Articles 099

饮器
Drinking Vessels 100

食器
Dining Utensils 110

容器
Containers 113

茶具
Tea Sets.. 116

装饰品
Ornaments.. 123

其他器形
Other Articles 128

中国金银器概述
Overview of China's Gold and Silver Articles

　　黄金和白银是古代最贵重的金属，古人对其开采利用的历史几乎与文明史同步。金银器，即用金、银制造的器具，拥有华美珍贵的质料与精致繁复的技艺，富丽堂皇，光灿辉耀。

Gold and silver are the most valuable metals in ancient times, when our ancestors started to exploit them since the civilization emerged. These palatial and flamboyant articles were made of colorful precious materials and by elaborate skills.

> 源远流长的金银文化

中国人对黄金和白银的认识和利用有着悠久的历史和光辉灿烂的文化。古代先民自从认识了金银，就将其应用于首饰装饰业、货币制造业和工艺品制造业等诸多领域中，打造出一件件精美绝伦的金银器，创造出了灿烂的金银文化。

> Long History of Gold and Silver Culture

The knowledge and utilization of the gold and silver has a long history in China and generated a brilliant culture. The ancient ancestors applied gold and silver into many fields like jewellery industry, monetary production, handicraft manufacturing and so on since they were discovered. With the countless exquisite

- **错银鎏金壶**

此壶扁圆形，直筒颈，圆口有盖，盖正中设置有半环形纽，肩部有对称的衔环，底为长方形圈足。此壶的纹饰精美，褐底白纹，壶盖、口沿和圈足鎏有一层黄灿灿的金色，与壶体银白纹样交相辉映。

Mixed Silver and Gilding Pot

This oval-shaped pot has a straight tube cover, round bottleneck with cap, semicircular knob in the center, balanced holding rings, rectangle-shaped bottom with ring foot. The decoration of this pot is exquisite, skewbald body embellished with gilding on the cap, bottle rim and ring foot, and the silver white pattern on the main body.

● 金碗
Gold Bowl

● 鎏金铜龙

龙是中国古代的祥瑞之兽，身长若蛇，有鳞似鱼，有角仿鹿，有爪似鹰，能翻江倒海，兴云布雨。因此在中国封建时代，龙是帝王的象征。

Gilding Bronze Dragon

Dragon is one of the auspicious divine beasts in ancient China. It has snake-like body with fish-like scales and deer-like horns and hawk-like claws. It has an overwhelming force. In Feudal Times of China the dragon is the symbol of the emperor.

在古代的中国，金银是高贵身份的象征。据《汉书》记载：帝王死后穿金缕玉衣，王侯、后妃等人穿银缕玉衣，公主等人穿铜缕玉

gold and silver articles forged, a gorgeous gold and silver culture was created.

Gold and silver are the symbol of the noble identity in ancient China. According to the record in the *Book of Han*, passed away emperors were buried in jade suits sewn with gold thread. Silver thread was used for high-ranking aristocrats and queens. Copper thread was used for princesses and so on. The jade burial suits were made of jade pieces joined with gold, silver or copper thread. Gold and silver articles even became the symbol of social status since the Tang Dynasty (618-907). For example, only the highest-rank officials could use gold dining utensils. The officials of sixth-rank and above could use silver dining utensils. Those under sixth-rand were not allowed to use silver ones.

Ancient Chinese adored the gold and silver to an ultimate level, especially for the gold. There were many old phrases relevant to "gold". For example, *Jade Sayings from a Gold Mouth*, describes the promises couldn't be broken. *As Strong as Gold* describes the firm city walls. *Golden Boy* refers to a smart cute boy and *Golden Branch* refers to a noble girl. *Lost in Gold and Drunk in Paper* means living a life of luxury and dissipation.

衣。这就是用金丝、银丝或铜丝把玉片连缀在一起制成葬服。从唐代开始，金银器更成为使用者等级地位的象征，如一品以下的官员不可以金做食器，六品以下的官员不可以银做食器等。

中国古人对金银极其崇拜，尤其黄金的地位更是至高无上。古代有很多词汇都与"金"字有关，如"金口玉言"形容承诺永不改变，"金科玉律"形容原则不容更改，"一刻千金"形容时间宝贵，"固若金汤"形容城池坚固不摧，"金童"指的是聪明可爱的男孩，"金枝"则指身份高贵的女孩，形容奢华而腐朽的生活即为"纸醉金迷"，形容一个人由坏向好的转变即为"浪子回头金不换"……

古人之所以如此崇拜金银，不仅仅因为其稀有，还由于他们相信使用金银器有益健康。中国古代会使用银针来检测食物是否有毒，这是由于银与许多的毒素能发生化学反应，毒素可使银变黑。此外，古人还利用白银来加速伤口愈合、净化水质及防腐保鲜等。

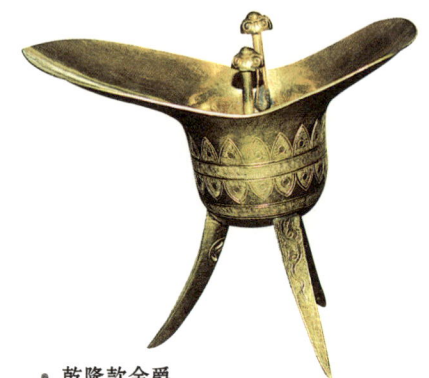

● 乾隆款金爵
爵为古代的一种饮酒器，在青铜器中较为多见，类似于后世的酒杯。
Gold *Jue* of Emperor Qianlong
Jue is a kind of ancient wine cup, which can be seen more as bronze articles.

Golden Rules means the principles are not susceptible to alteration. And there also are *A Thousand Pieces of Gold Can't Buy a Moment* and *A Prodigal Who Has Mended His Ways Is More Precious Than Gold*...

The ancients adored gold and silver not only due to their rareness, but also because they believed gold and silver are wholesome for users. Ancient Chinese used to test food with silver needle to see if it's poisoned. Because silver can produce chemical reaction and turn black when met with great majority of poisons. Besides, the ancients also used silver

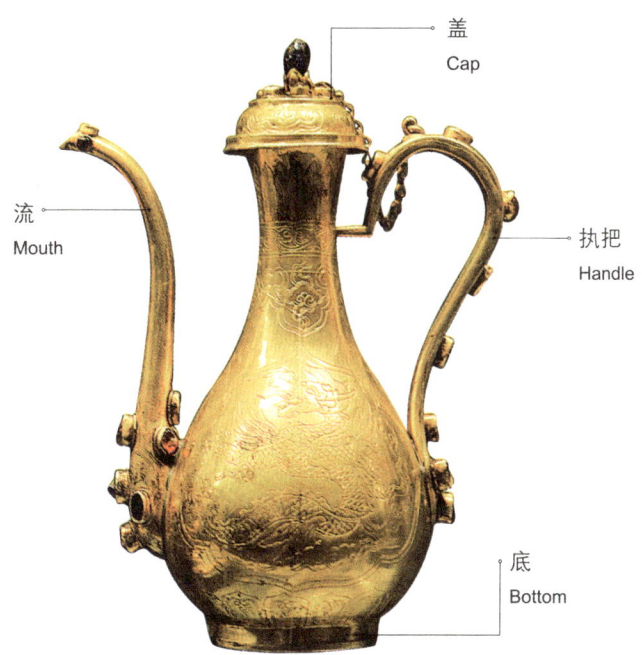

盖 Cap
流 Mouth
执把 Handle
底 Bottom

- **嵌宝石金刻龙纹壶**

  此壶束颈，鼓腹，圈足，盖以链与柄相系。壶盖、壶颈及近底部錾刻有蕉叶纹、卷草纹、如意云头纹、莲瓣纹等纹样；腹部两侧火焰形开光内刻四爪翼龙两条。盖顶、流、把上皆镶嵌有红蓝宝石，共27颗。

  Jeweled Gold Pot with Carved Dragon

  Collected bottleneck, drum abdomen, ring foot, the cap was connect to the handle with chain. Banana-leaf, grass, cloud and lotus-petal patterns carved on the cap, bottleneck and near bottom; two four-claw dragons separately carved on the both flame-shaped abdomen flanks. 27 rubies and sapphires are inlaid on the cap, chain, and handle.

除此之外，金银器珍贵的材质及其所散发出的璀璨夺目的光泽和其精美的工艺，都是人们喜爱它们的原因。

for healing wound, purifying water and preventing decay and so on.

Beyond that, people are fond of gold and silver articles also because of their bright and dazzling gloss, precious materials and the fine craft.

古人对金银的开采

据唐代史料记载，中国古代的先民寻找金银矿是根据植物来辨别的，即山上如果有野生的葱，其下多半会有银矿；山上如果生长有冬青树，其下多半会有金矿。经现代科学验证，土壤中含有不同的金属元素会影响植物的生长。宋代史料记载，如果掘地时遇到"粉子石"，此石一头焦黑，则表明其下有金矿；如果遇到一堆堆微带褐色的小石头，则其下有银矿。

古人开采金银矿的方法主要为淘洗法和地下井巷挖掘法两种。淘洗法主要用于砂金的提取；而地下井巷挖掘法则适用于山金及银矿的开采。

Gold and Silver Exploitation in Ancient Times

In the historical records of the Tang Dynasty (618-907), the ancient Chinese searched for gold and silver mines through surveying the vegetative cover. The silver mines usually exist in the mountains where wild green shallots grow; the gold mines can be found in the mountains where Common Hollies grow. The modern science researched that the metallic elements in the soil can affect the growing of plants. In the historical records of the Song Dynasty (960-1279), in exploitation finding *Fenzi* stone, which is burned black on one side, means there would be a gold mine underneath; finding piles of little rocks in light brown, there might be silver mine below.

The ancients' methods of gold and silver mines exploiting can be mainly divided into elutriation method and underground mining method. The elutriation method was used to pick up gulch-gold; the underground mining method was used in the exploiting of mountain gold and silver mines.

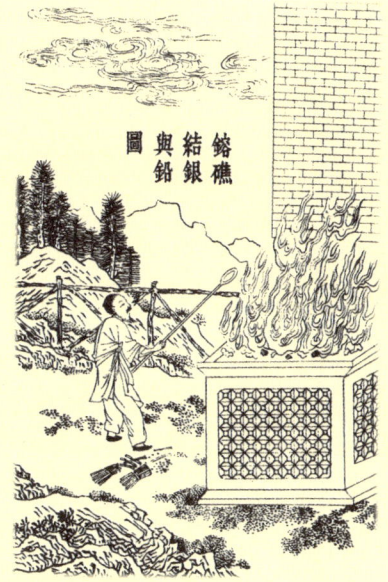

- **《天工开物》中古人冶炼金银的绘图**

  《天工开物》为明代科学家宋应星所著，是一部综合性的科学技术著作。书中收录了机械、陶瓷、纸、兵器、火药、纺织、采煤、榨油等生产技术，其中包括金属的铸锻过程。

  Pictures of Ancients' Smelting of Gold and Silver from *Exploitation of the Works of Nature*

  Exploitation of the Works of Nature was written by Song Yingxing, a famous scientist in the Ming Dynasty (1368-1644). It was a comprehensive science and technology work, embodied technologies like machinery, ceramics, paper, weaponry, powder, spinning, coal mining, and oil manufacture and so on, including casting processes of metals.

> 历代金银器的特点

中国的金银文化绵久而辉煌，早在距今约三千多年的商周时期就已出现了黄金制品，春秋战国时期则开始了对白银制品的使用。逐渐地，金银器不仅代表财富，而且还被用来作为身份地位和富贵等级的标志，成为皇家贵族的珍宠。

商周金银器

中国的金制品出现的时间比银器要早。据考古发现，商代时已有黄金制品了，其分布范围主要是以商周文化为中心的中原地区，以及商周王朝北部、西北部和偏西南的少数民族地区。这一时期的金器，形制工艺简单，器形小巧，纹饰少见，且大多为装饰品。

商代的黄金制品多为金箔、金

> Characteristics of the Gold and Silver Articles in Different Dynasties

The history of China's gold and silver culture is long and glory. Gold articles emerged about three thousand years ago, in the Shang and Zhou dynasties. Silver articles were put in use in the Spring and Autumn and Warring States periods. Gradually, the gold and silver articles not only represented the wealth, but also be the symbol of social status and wealth levels, and were favored by the imperial families and nobilities.

Gold and Silver Articles of the Shang and Zhou Dynasties

The gold articles in China emerged earlier than the silver articles. According to excavations, China began to make gold articles during the Shang Dynasty (1600 B.C.-1046 B.C.). The distribution

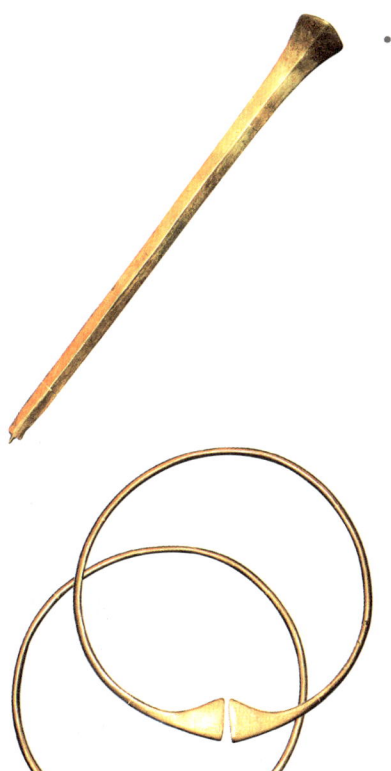

• 金笄

笄是古代用于盘发挽髻的簪。早在新石器时代，中国妇女已用骨制的发笄。在中国古代，女子插笄，标志着成年，需举行仪式，称为"笄礼"。此金笄器身两面不一，一面光滑，一面有脊，截断面呈纯三角形，头部宽，尾部逐渐变窄，便于穿插。其尾端有一长约0.4厘米的榫状结构，可能是用于镶嵌其他的装饰品。

Gold Hairpin

Ji is kind of the hairpin in ancient times. Early in the Neolithic Period, the Chinese women started to use hairpins made of bones. In ancient China, women wearing *Ji* indicated they grew up, an adult woman's coming-of-age ceremony was known as *Ji* Ceremony. The two sides of this Gold *Ji* are different, one is smooth and the other is backbone-raised. The truncation face is pure triangle, broad head, gradually narrows down to the end, easy to wear. There is a 0.4 centimeters long tenon shape structure on its end, might be designed for other inlays.

• 金臂钏

臂钏是古代一种套在上臂的环形首饰，一般为女性佩戴，能够表现女性上臂丰满浑圆的魅力。

Gold Arm Bracelet

Arm bracelets were usually worn by ancient women, showing the charm of their chubby upper arms.

叶和金片，主要用于器物装饰。这一时期的金器中最令人瞩目的是四川广汉三星堆出土的一批金器，不仅数量多，而且形制别具一格。当

range covered the Ancient Central Plain Area where the Shang and Zhou Culture generated, and the northern, northwestern and southwestern areas of the Shang and Zhou dynasties where the ethnic groups lived. The gold articles in this period were simple in craft, shaped tiny and had few patterns, mostly were adornment.

The gold articles in the Shang Dynasty were mostly made of gold foil, gold leaf and gold plaque, and were mainly used to decorate articles. The most important gold articles in this period were the ones excavated from the Sanxingdui site in Guanghan City, Sichuan Province, not only because of the number, but also for their peculiar shapes. Of course, as the bronze manufacturing was in its noontide

然，商周处于青铜铸造业的巅峰时期，所以处于滥觞阶段的金银器工艺并没有对时代产生较大影响。

in the Shang and Zhou dynasties, the new born gold and silver articles didn't generate great influence.

三星堆金器

三星堆遗址位于四川广汉南兴镇，于1980年开始发掘。三星堆文明是中国长江流域早期文明（蜀文化）的代表，被誉为"长江文明之源"。

三星堆出土的文物包括中原地区常见的大型礼器、兵器及大量青铜人物雕像。此外，三星堆出土的金器也同样精美绝伦，不仅工艺精湛，还被赋予高度的政治、宗教意义。其中当属金面罩、金臂钏、金笄、金杖等最有特点，由此不难看出，那时人们已经开始把金制品用作装饰物了。

Sanxingdui Gold Articles

The Sanxingdui site locates in Nanxing Town, Guanghan City, Sichuan Province, the excavation started in 1980. The Sanxingdui Civilization is a delegate of the China's early civilization in the Yangtze River basin (the Shu Culture), as well as the known "The Origin of Civilization in the Yangtze River".

The unearthed cultural relics from Sanxingdui include large sacrificial vessels, weapons and vast of bronze statue of human, which were common in the Central Plains Area. Again, these gold articles not only are exquisite beyond compare for its craftsmanship, but also possess high political and religious significances. The most significant articles are gold mask, gold arm bracelet, gold hairpin and gold truncheon. Therefore, it is pretty sure that people started using gold articles as ornament since then.

● 金面罩（图片提供：全景正片）

金面罩与青铜人面像相结合，用纯金皮模压而成，眉眼镂空，鼻部凸起，贴于青铜头像的面部。

Gold Mask

This gold mask is mould pressed of pure gold, with hollowed eyes and brows and bulged nose, attached to the face of the bronze statues.

春秋战国金银器

春秋战国时期，金银器的制作工艺已达到了很高的水平，制作出来的器具或饰品极为美观精巧，形制和花纹是在青铜工艺基础上发展起来的。从出土的实物来看，这一时期出现了金柄铁剑、金银带钩、金银容器等极具特色的器物。

战国以前，中国金银制品大多为形制小巧的装饰品，罕有容器或其他器皿出现。战国以后，尤其是在远离中原的东南地区，逐渐形成

● **金带钩**
带钩是一种扣绊革带的构件，也可用以悬系武器、玺印、铜镜、钱袋等物。由于系在人们视觉最集中的腰际，因而造型和制作工艺极受重视。

Gold Belt Hook
It was used to fasten the leather belt worn around the waist, as well as to hook weapon, seal, bronze mirror and moneybag. Since the waist is the most conspicuous part of the body, the appearance and craftsmanship are regarded highly important.

Gold and Silver Articles of the Spring and Autumn and Warring States Periods

The craftsmanship of gold and silver products had reached a high level in the Spring and Autumn and Warring States periods (770 B.C.-221 B.C.). The articles made in this period are extremely beautiful and ingenious. Their shapes and patterns were developed from bronze techniques. According to excavations, iron sword with gold hilt, gold and silver belt hook, gold and silver containers emerged in this period.

Most of the gold and silver articles made before the Warring States Period (475 B.C.- 221 B.C.) are small elegant ornament, with few containers and other household utensils. Since the Warring States Period, especially in the southeastern area far away from the Central Plains, the function of the gold and silver articles gradually distinct from the Central Plain and the northern area. The gold and silver articles of northern area and remote ethnic minority areas are mainly discovered in the tombs of the nobles of the Eastern Zhou Dynasty (770 B.C.-256 B.C.) and the nomadic people in the Warring States Period

了与中原、北方在金银器使用功能上的差异。北方和边远少数民族地区的金银器以内蒙古、新疆、陕西等地出土最多，主要发现于东周贵

located in Inner Mongolia Autonomous Region, Xinjiang Uygur Autonomous Region, Shaanxi Province, etc. Most of them are ornaments and horse gears decorations. The quantity is small but

器盖装饰有绳纹和用回旋线条组成的云雷纹，纹理看上去细如毫发，其铸工之精，远远超过同一时期的中原铜器。

The cap is decorated with string pattern and cloud thunder pattern composed with swing lines. The texture is hair-like fine and the fineness of casting technique is far more advanced than the Central Plains' bronze articles at that time.

器盖中央有4个短柱连接的环状捉手。

A loop handle with 4 short cylinders attaches to the center of the cap.

器底有3个"S"形的凤头形足。

It has three sigmoid feet in the shape of phoenix head in the bottom.

器盖与盏身装饰有繁缛细密的蟠螭纹，蟠螭形态各异，既有单体的，也有作多体虬结的。

The cap and body are decorated with complex dragon-snake patterns in different shapes and numbers.

• **曾侯乙墓出土的金盏**（图片提供：FOTOE）

此金盏通高11厘米，重2150克，含金量98%，是已知先秦金器中最大的一件。此盏造型端庄稳重，装饰奇特，铸造工艺极为复杂，捉手、盖、身、足分铸，即器身与附件分别做成，然后再合范浇铸或焊接成器，这与当时青铜器的铸造方法相同。

Gold Calix Discovered in the Tomb of Marquis Yi of Zeng State

This gold calix is 11 centimeters high, 2150 grams weight, known as the largest gold article before the Qin Dynasty (221 B.C.-206 B.C.) whose gold content is 98%. The appearance of this calix is steady, with fancy decoration and complex casting technique. The handle, cap, body and feet are casted separately and then casted or welded together. This method is the same with the bronze casting at that time.

族墓和战国时期游牧民族的贵族墓中，以首饰与马具上的饰件居多，虽金银器皿为数不多，但工艺上已达到较为完善的程度。南方地区出土的金银器数量虽然不多，但却十分引人注目。其中最为重要的发现，当属湖北省曾侯乙墓出土的一批金器。

the craftsmanship is rather perfect. The unearthed gold and silver articles found in southern area are rare but very noticeable. The most important discovery is a hoard of gold articles uncovered from the Tomb of Marquis Yi of Zeng State in Hubei Province.

- **鎏金银琵琶形带钩**

  战国中后期，带钩的制作与使用进入到了鼎盛期，新兴的琵琶形带钩空前盛行，在钩身上铸出浮雕式兽面纹，立体感甚强。

  Gilding Silver Belt Hook in the Shape of Chinese Lute

  The producing and using of belt hook reached its peak in the later Warring States Period. The newly emerged Chinese lute shaped belt hook became extremely popular. The animal face patterns casted in relief on its back enhance the third dimension.

- **嵌松石云纹方豆**

  方豆是春秋战国时期一种方斗形的豆盘，其盘为方形，下部有柄和座。此件方豆通体饰云纹，杂嵌绿松石。

  Square Dou Inlaid with Turquoise and Inlaid Clouds Pattern

  Square Dou is a type of ancient stemmed cup or bowl in the Spring and Autumn and Warring States periods, with a square plate, a handle and a base in the bottom. The whole body has cloud pattern, inlaid with turquoise.

- **错金铜匜**

  匜是古代一种盥洗器，用于洗手洗脸。

  Bronze *Yi* (Basin)Inlaid with Gold

  Yi is kind of basin for washing face and hands in ancient times.

金环铁削

削是古代一种工具，春秋战国和秦汉时用来除去书写在木牍或竹简上的错字，形状尖锋锐利，截面呈弯月形。

Iron Cutter with Gold Ring

These cutters were used to cut off the wrongly written characters on wood tablets or bamboo slips in the Spring and Autumn Period, the Warring States Period and the Qin and Han dynasties. They are shaped like meniscus and very sharp.

银座玉琮

琮是中国古代用于祭祀的玉质筒状物，大多内圆外方。此银座玉琮光素无纹，上覆圆形银盖，顶心粘嵌扁圆弧凸水晶一枚，盖沿一周透穿四组八个小孔；下配四鹰足鎏金银座，鹰作张口、展翅、站立状。

Jade *Cong* with Silver Base

Cong is a rectangular piece of jade with hole in middle used for sacrifice in ancient China. This jade *Cong* with silver base is plain with silver round cover on the top, an oval-shaped crystal is embedded in the center of the cover, and the cover was penetrated for 4 times into eight apertures. Four eagle shaped gilding silver feet in the bottom, the appearance of the eagles are mouth open, standing and ready to fly.

最早的金币和银币

　　早在商代时，黄金就已开始作为货币出现，战国时期则更多地用黄金论价。白银货币则始于西汉，到宋代时成为主要的币材。

　　战国时期的金币有金版与金饼两种形式。金版，即外观扁平的版形金币，大都呈规则或不规则的长方形或方形。金饼，即形如饼状的金币，呈不规则的圆形或椭圆形，其上多钤印文字或字符，饼面中心微凸，底面中心微凹。金版和金饼在使用时会根据需要切割成小块，然后用天平称量支付。银币的出现略晚于金币，形态有贝、铲、版三种。

The Earliest Gold and Silver Coins

Gold started to be used as currency as early as the Shang Dynasty (1600 B.C.-1046 B.C.), and most of the price determined in the Warring States Period (475 B.C.-221 B.C.) were by gold. The silver coins appeared since the Western Han Dynasty (206 B.C.-25 A.D.), and became the major currency material in the Song Dynasty (960-1279).

    The gold coins in the Warring States Period can be divided into 2 forms: the gold board and gold plate. The board-shaped gold coins are mostly in regularly-shaped or irregularly-shaped rectangle or square. The plate-shaped gold coins are irregular round or ellipse, mostly sealed with characters, the center of the positive side bulges slightly and the center of the other side is concave. When using them, the gold board and gold plate should all be cut into small pieces according to the need and paid after weighed on a balance. The silver coins came out after the gold ones, which can be separated by their shapes into shell, spade and flat.

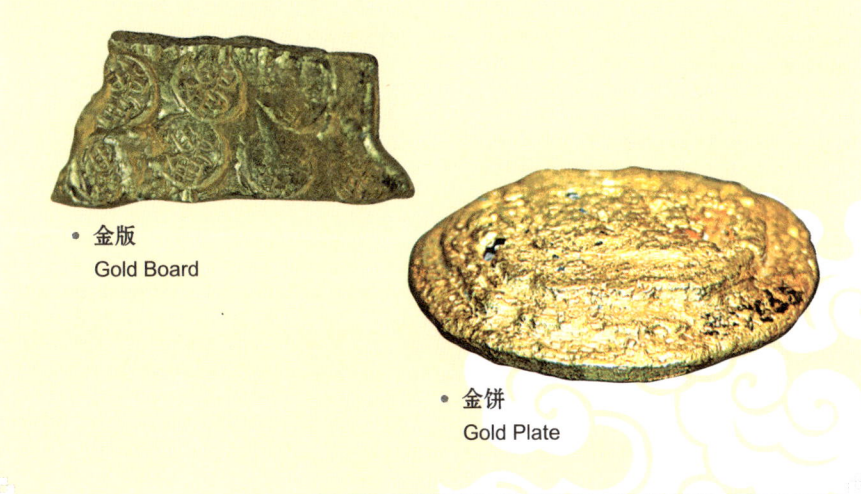

• 金版
Gold Board

• 金饼
Gold Plate

秦汉金银器

    秦汉时代是中国历史上的第一次大一统时期，金银器具风靡一时。这一时期青铜器衰败，铁器兴盛，金银器渐渐脱离了铜器的附属

Gold and Silver Articles of the Qin and Han Dynasties

The great unification for the first time in Chinese history was achieved during the Qin and Han dynasties. and the gold and silver articles became popular for a time. At that time the bronze declined while the

- 金银针

金银针是中国古代的一种医疗器具，用于放血和针灸。

Gold and Silver Needles

Gold and Silver Needle is a kind of medical equipment in ancient China, used for acupuncture and bloodletting.

- 金五铢

金五铢是中国方孔圆钱中最早的黄金铸币，含金量达95%。此币边廓坚挺精整，钱面穿上有一横划，上铸"五铢"二字，形体颀长。

Gold *Wu-Zhu*

The Gold *Wu-Zhu* is the first square-hole round gold coin of China, with 95% gold content. This coin has a neat edge, a transverse line and characters of *Wu and Zhu* in tall shape on the surface.

地位而走上独立发展的道路，成为一个专门的手工艺门类。

秦汉时期的金银器发展与封建统治者的重视密不可分。秦汉的君王认为，使用黄金制成的饮食器皿，可以延年益寿、长生不死。因此，金银器的使用仅限于宫禁之内。

秦代金银器出土实物较少，但两汉时期金银器的数量和质量普遍提高，特别是制作工艺开始向细工方向发展，掐丝、焊接、镶嵌等金

ironware flourished, the gold and silver articles gradually separated themselves from being the subsidiary of the bronze articles and became a specialized handicraft.

The development of the gold and silver articles in the Qin and Han dynasties owed to the spoiling from the feudal rulers. The emperors of that time thought that using gold articles for food and drink can prolong one's life and cheat death. For that reason, the usage of the gold and silver articles was limited within the palace.

- "五威司命领军"银印

秦汉以后，官印的材质有了严格的等级区分，金银印只适用于皇太子、诸侯王、王后、列侯、丞相、大将军等人。

Silver Seal of an Official

Since the Qin and Han dynasties, the materials of the official seals were strictly connected with the social estate system. Gold and silver seals could be only used by the crown prince, vassal king, queen, marquis, prime minister and senior general.

- 鎏金蚕

此蚕蚕体饱满，形象逼真，制作精致。在西汉时，中国的养蚕业就已十分兴盛，西汉丝织品不仅畅销国内，而且能途经西亚行销中亚和欧洲，这条商路即驰名于世界的丝绸之路。

Gilding Silkworm

This silkworm has a plump and vivid appearance, the craft is delicate. Sericulture was prosperous in China during the Western Han Dynasty. Silk fabrics were in great demand in the country and can be sold via West Asia to Middle Asia and Europe as well. This trade route is the world famous Silk Road.

- 龙凤纹银铺首

铺首是中国古代镶嵌在门上的装饰，一般以金属制作，作虎、龟、蛇等形状。

Silver *Pushou* with Dragon and Phoenix Patter

Pu shou is one of the decorations inlaid in the door in ancient China, generally made of metal, appearing as the shape of tiger, turtle, snake and so on.

- 银药具

Silver Medicine Utensil

银细工都较为成熟。当时制作的金版、金王冠等都非常精良，所表现出的奢豪堂皇的造型及繁缛富丽的装饰都令人叹为观止。两汉时期，金银器的基本工艺都已形成，从而使金银器的制作从青铜器制作的传统工艺中彻底分离出来，为唐宋金银器的繁荣打下了坚实的基础。

The number of the gold and silver articles from the Qin Dynasty (221 B.C.-206 B.C.) to be excavated is small, but the quality and quantity generally became better when it went to the Han Dynasty. Especially the craftsmanship had developed into a more refined one, and filigree, welding, inlaid and other techniques were mature. The plates or crowns made of gold at that time were excellent, which amazed people with luxurious appearances and magnificent decorations. In the Han Dynasty, all the basic handicrafts of the gold and silver articles had been developed and separated from the traditional bronze manufacture completely, which laid a solid foundation for the booming of the gold and silver articles in the Tang and Song dynasties.

金缕玉衣

金缕玉衣是汉代皇帝和高级贵族死后穿用的殓服。玉衣即用玉片制成，玉片的角上穿孔，用黄金制成的丝缕编缀，故称"金缕玉衣"。据史料记载，汉代帝王下葬都用"珠襦玉匣"，形如铠甲，用金丝连接，这种玉匣就是人们日常所说的"金缕玉衣"。

Jade Burial Suit

Jade Burial Suit was a kind of shroud which worn by the emperors and high aristocrats after their death in the Han Dynasty (206 B.C.-220 A.D.). The suits were made of thousands of pieces of jade. They were joined with gold thread through tiny holes in the corners of each piece, that's why it's called Jade Burial Suit. According to history books, emperors of the Han Dynasty were all buried in jade suits.

● 金缕玉衣

此件金缕玉衣为西汉靖王刘胜的殓服，共用2498片玉片，玉片为岫岩玉，金丝约1100克。整体由头部、上衣、手套、裤筒、鞋五部分组成，各部分可彼此分离，并附有九窍塞。依汉制，作为诸侯王的刘胜只能着"银缕"玉衣，但他却着"金缕"，可能和西汉时"玉衣"尚未定制有关。

Jade Burial Suit

This jade burial suit is made for Prince Liu Sheng of the Western Han Dynasty. It is made of 2498 pieces of *Xiuyan* Jade and about 1100 grams gold thread. The ensembles was composed with 5 parts, the head, upper garment, gloves, trousers and shoes. Each part can be separated. Attached with the suit, are jade *Jiuqiao Sai* (nine orifice plugs used to block up a corpse). Jade suits were made in accordance with rigid rules. In the Han Dynasty, silver thread was used for princes like Liu Sheng, but he was buried in gold-thread-jointed jade suit which may relate to the fact that jade suits were not customized in the Western Han Dynasty.

魏晋南北朝金银器

魏晋南北朝时期，中原战乱频繁，社会经济遭到了严重的破坏，金银矿兴废无常。但南方社会相对来说比较稳定，经济有了较大发展，对外

Gold and Silver Articles of Three Kingdoms, Jin Dynasty, Southern and Northern Dynasties

In the Three Kingdoms, Jin Dynasty, Southern and Northern dynasties (220-589), frequent wars in the Central

交流进一步扩大，金银器等艺术品也得到了前所未有的发展。

据考古发现，这一时期的金银器数量较多，但以小型饰物为主，包括头饰、手饰、佩饰等，其中以头饰最引人注目。这一时期的金银饰物在风格上简朴平实，少有华丽的装饰，这是当时人们崇尚自然的反映。

同时，从中亚、西亚输入中国的金银器及装饰品数量颇丰；西方的形制和制作工艺在这一时期的饰物与容器上都有反映。总的来说，这一时期的金银器既继承了秦汉时期的传统，又汲取了各民族以及西方国家金银制作工艺的精华。外国

- 鎏金蟠龙环
  Gilding Ring in the Shaped of Curled-up Dragon

Plains seriously damaged the social economy, while gold and silver mines were developed and abandoned all the time. Respectively speaking, the society was steady in the south, the economy developed significantly and the outside communication expanded further, as a result, the work of arts like gold and silver articles blossomed well unprecedentedly.

According to the archaeological discovery, the quantity of gold and silver articles in this period was huge, which mainly were small articles for personal adornment like head wears, hand wears, baldrics and so on. Among them the head wears were the most remarkable. The gold and silver articles of this period were simple in style, barely can find luxuriant decorations, for that the people of this period upheld the natural phenomena.

In the meantime, a lot of gold and silver articles and decorations were imported to China from Middle Asia and West Asia. Western styles and crafts can be found in the articles and containers of this period. In general, the gold and silver articles of this period not only inherited the tradition of the Qin and Han dynasties, but also adopted the essences of the technique of processing gold and

- **"晋归义氏王"金印**

  魏晋南北朝时期，由于王朝更替频繁，官印的数量激增，原本严格的等级制度也大大减弱，许多将军级以下的官员也开始使用金印，但往往以鎏金制成。

  Gold Seal Issued by the Government of the Western Jin Dynasty to the Leader of a Tribe

  As the dynasties replaced frequently during the Wei, Jin, Southern and Northern dynasties, the number of seals grew rapidly and the previous strict social estate system was weakened. Many officers who were lower than generals started to use gold seals, but the seals they used were often gilding.

- **鎏金铜车饰**

  Gilding Copper Chariot Ornament

- **梁元帝金银竹笔**

  Gold, Silver and Bamboo Brush Pens owned by Emperor Yuan of Liang

● 马头鹿角形金饰件

此饰件轮廓清楚，马头部狭长，眼睛凸出，两颊下收，鼻尖镶白色料石，鼻梁上端用狭薄条金片圈一菱形装饰，桃形眉饰镶有料石，呈淡蓝色，日光下泛雪青色，眉梢上端另加一对圆圈纹。鹿角作三枝并立向上，中间一枝不作分枝，枝干下部饰一周鱼子纹，每枝悬挂有桃形叶片。

Gold Ornament in the Shape of Horse Head with Antlers

This ornament has a clear outline with the horse head long and narrow, eyes bulged, cheeks drawback and white stone inlaid on horse nose. A narrow thin strip golden piece decorates the upper of the bridge of the nose, peach-shaped eyebrows inlaid with nattier blue stones, which appear violet color in the sunlight, and a pair of circle patterns on the upper end of the eyebrow tips. Three antlers are upward side by side. The middle one has no branches, and the lower part of the branches are decorated with a circle of roe pattern, with peach-shaped leaves attached to each branch.

金银制品相继输入中国，引发了统治阶层对传统金银器造型艺术审美视角的转换，从而对中国金银制品制作加工产生了巨大的影响。

魏晋南北朝时期，佛教在中国兴盛，建造了许多寺院，同时铸造了大量的佛像和其他佛教用具，多用金或鎏金。这一时期金银器的制造大多与一些信仰联系在一起。

隋唐金银器

隋唐是中国封建社会的强盛时期，统一的多民族国家进一步发展，社会经济呈现出前所未有的繁荣景象。统治阶级为了追求豪华的生活，

silver from the other ethnic groups and western countries. The import of the gold and silver articles changed the aesthetic perspective of the ruling class toward the traditional gold and silver arts, which significantly influenced and changed the manufacture of China's gold and silver products.

In the Wei, Jin, Southern and Northern dynasties, the Buddhism was thriving in China, and many temples were built. In the meantime, a mass of josses and other Buddhist appliances in gold or gilding were made. As a result, the manufacture of the gold and silver articles in this period was often connected to some religions.

唐代酒文化与金银器

唐代的饮酒之风盛行，上至帝后王臣、下至平民百姓，无不以纵酒豪饮为乐事。唐人在饮酒时，总要行酒令（筵宴上助兴取乐的游戏），以增加饮酒的乐趣。豪饮之风使唐代的金银饮器大为兴盛，如今的出土物中有各式银碗、银杯、金碗、金杯、银盒、银罐、银壶等。

The Wine Culture and the Gold and Silver Articles in the Tang Dynasty

Drinking was popular in the Tang Dynasty (618-907). People from imperial nobles to common folks were all fond of drinking. They usually play wager games during feast to have more fun. This culture flourished the gold and silver drinking articles of the Tang Dynasty. Various gold and silver bowls and cups, silver boxes, jars, and pots were excavated.

● 凤首银执壶
Silver Jar in the Shape of Phoenix Head

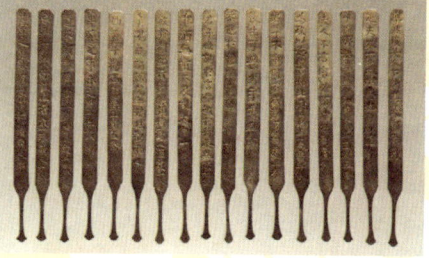

● 银涂金论语酒令筹

这批从唐代银器窖藏出土的酒令筹共50枚，均呈长方形，下端收拢为细柄状，每枚正面都刻有行酒辞令，字内鎏金；令辞上半段采自《论语》语句，下半段是酒令的具体内容。

Gilding Silver Slips Inlaid Sayings from *The Analects* Used in Drinking Games

This batch excavated from the Silver Ware Kiln of the Tang Dynasty has 50 pieces of drinking game chips, all in rectangle shape, the lower end drawn in thin handle. Each slip bears a saying from *The Analects* and inscribed beneath are some game rules.

• 赤金走龙

中国古代的龙纹或龙饰大多气势磅礴，可唐代的赤金走龙却小巧玲珑，朴素平实，据推测可能是祭祀仪式中所用的法器，也可能是皇家的装饰品。此件赤金走龙是先用金丝掐编出龙的身体，然后插上尾巴和角，最后用錾子錾出鱼鳞纹。

Pure Gold Walking Dragon

Most ancient China's dragon patterns or decorations were of great momentum, but this Pure Gold Walking Dragon is small and simple, which was guessed to be a sacrifice instrument or royal decoration. This dragon was first made the body with gold wire, then attached with tail and horn, at last carved with scale pattern.

大量使用金银作为饰物，从而促进了隋唐金银器手工业的发展。

隋王朝历时较短，迄今为止仅发现一些金杯、金手镯、金项链、金戒指、银杯、银筷、银勺等。

唐代奢靡享乐之风盛行，金光闪闪、银光熠熠的金银器，凭借其华丽的外观和浓郁的文化气息，成为展示大唐王朝富丽堂皇、灿烂夺目的标志之一，而使用金银器也成

Gold and Silver Articles of the Sui and Tang Dynasties

The Sui and Tang dynasties were the most powerful period in China's feudal society, the unified multiethnic country developed to a higher level, and the social economy showed unprecedented prosperity. The ruling class pursued luxurious life and slathered gold and silver as articles, which promoted the development of the gold and silver handicraft industry of that time.

The Sui Dynasty (581-618) was short in time, so to this day only a small numbers of gold and silver articles had been found, like gold cups, gold bracelets, gold necklaces, gold rings, silver cups, silver chopsticks, silver spoons and so on.

The atmosphere of the Tang Dynasty (618-907) was extravagant and hedonic; the shiny gold and silver articles with beautiful appearances and strong cultural deposits became one of the symbols of magnificence and brilliance of the Tang Dynasty. And gold and silver wares became popular in the noble estate. Meanwhile, the opened empire absorbed and accepted foreign culture easily and the culture communication between China and the western countries

- 银石榴药罐

此药罐是古代用来熬药的器具，可以作为简单的蒸馏器。

Silver Gallipot in the Shape of Pomegranate

This gallipot was used to brew liquid preparation with medicinal herbs in ancient times, which can be regarded as a simple distiller.

- 鎏金双鱼纹银碗

此鎏金银碗，将立体的鱼粘于碗的底部，双鱼并列遨游，宽叶六瓣折枝花围绕，花纹全部鎏金，无比精美。这件银碗的造型、纹饰及錾刻方法均与宫廷作坊的做法不同，应为民间作坊所制，具有鲜明的地方特色。

Gilding Silver Bowl with Double Fish Pattern

This gilding silver bowl is with tridimensional fish attached to the bottom. Two fish swim side by side and are surrounded by wide blade injured hexapetalous flowers. The modeling, pattern and carving of this bowl are all different from those in the imperial workshop, which should be made by a folk workshop and have distinctive regional features.

- 錾花花口金碗

Gold Bowl with Flower Edged Mouth and Carved Patterns

- 鎏金串枝花银盒

Gilding Silver Box with Bunch Flower Pattern

为贵族阶层高贵身份的一种炫耀。同时，开放的大唐帝国以宽松的心态吸收和接受外来文化，中西方文化交流更加频繁，大量金银器流入中国，西方盛行的锤鍱技艺也已被唐代工匠全面掌握。唐代在金银器制作工艺方面，既善于总结和继承前人的成就，又开阔思路，吸收并消化外来文化中的丰富营养，因此唐代金银器的技艺之高超，花纹之精美，品种之繁多，均是前所未有的。纵观唐代金银器，不仅种类繁多，而且纹饰极为丰富，这些纹饰与器形一样，具有强烈的时代特点和风格。通过这些金银器，可以感受到唐代现实生活的五彩缤纷和文化艺术的欣欣向荣。可以说，中国古代金银器皿是在唐代及其以后兴盛起来，并且代表了金属工艺的最高水平。

was more frequent, so great numbers of gold and silver articles were imported to China and the hammer skill which was popular in the western world had been mastered by the craftsmen of the Tang Dynasty. The craftsmanship of the gold and silver articles from the Tang Dynasty combined the traditional achievement and the foreign culture together; the skills, patterns and varieties of the articles reached the peak of history. The gold and silver articles from the Tang Dynasty had wide varieties, lavish patterns, possessing strong characteristics and styles of that time. We can feel the colorful life and the flourishing art of culture through these gold and silver articles. It can be said that the prosperity of ancient China's gold and silver articles started since the Tang Dynasty, which by then represented the highest level of metal craft.

"满城尽带黄金甲"的来历

"满城尽带黄金甲"出自唐代黄巢的《咏菊》一诗,全诗如下:

待到秋来九月八,

我花开后百花杀。

冲天香阵透长安,

满城尽带黄金甲。

这首诗讲的是唐代末年黄巢率领农民起义军进攻国都长安(今陕西西安)的情景。唐代末年,朝政混乱,百姓的生活越来越困苦,从而引发了大规模的农民战争。公元880年,起义军首领黄巢带领六十万大军,浩浩荡荡地攻入长安,朝野上下惊慌失措,皇帝更是逃往成都,来不及逃走的官员则全部投降。然而没过多久,朝廷重新调集兵马,反过来包围长安,打败了起义军。公元884年,黄巢英勇牺牲。

Origin of *The Full City Takes Gold to the Utmost*

It was originated from the poem *Ode to the Chrysanthemum* by Huang Chao of the Tang Dynasty.

Wait until an autumn to come to September eight, all flowers withered while my flowers blossom; fragrances sweep deeply through Chang-an, the full city takes gold to the utmost.

This poem described the scene that Huang Chao command the farmer rebellion to sweep the capital Chang'an (today's Xi'an City of Shaanxi Province) in the last period of the Tang Dynasty. In the last years of the Tang Dynasty, the state affairs were in chaos, and the hard life of the people caused large scale of peasant war. In 880, the leader of the rebel Huang Chao led six hundred thousand troops broke into Chang'an. The court was in panic and the emperor escaped to Chengdu, the left officers who didn't make to escape all surrendered.

But soon later, the imperial court reassembled forces and besieged Chang'an, defeated the rebel. Huang Chao gave up his life heroically in 884.

宋元金银器

从唐代晚期开始，金银器逐渐走入民间。宋代以后，金银器全面世俗化、商业化，以至普通百姓之家，及至酒楼等，都能无所顾忌地使用金银器，这使金银器的发展呈现多元化趋势。这一时期的金银器虽不及前朝的宏放气魄，但其风格却让人眼前一亮。与前朝相比，宋代金银器的造型玲珑奇巧、新颖雅

Gold and Silver Articles of the Song and Yuan Dynasties

The gold and silver articles were introduced into the folk since the later period of the Tang Dynasty (618-907). After the Song Dynasty (960-1279), the gold and silver articles achieved secularization and commercialization, even the taverns and ordinary people can use gold and silver articles without any limit, so the multiplication tendency

• 象纽莲盖银注子

注子是中国古代的酒壶，多以金属或瓷制成。宋代金银器普遍采用了立雕装饰和浮雕凸花工艺，立体感更加鲜明，这是宋代金银工匠的创举。

Silver *Zhuzi* (Wine Pot) with Elephant Knob and Lotus Cap

Zhuzi was the wine pot in ancient China, mostly made of metal or ceramic. The gold and silver articles of the Song Dynasty widely adopted stereo lithography and relief raising crafts for the more vivid three-dimension, which was the pioneering work of the craftsmen in the Song Dynasty.

• 铜镜和银镜架

此银镜架为折合式，分为前后两个支架，后架上部镂雕凤凰戏牡丹纹，框沿为如意式，顶端立雕有流云葵花纹。

Bronze Mirror and Silver Stand

The folding silver stand has two supports in front and back. The upper part of the back support is pierced with phoenix and peony pattern, and the rims are *Ruyi* type with a stereoscopic carving of cloud and sunflower pattern on the top.

- 银槎杯

槎，即树杈。槎杯即把杯作为树杈的形态，杂乱的树枝巧妙地顺应了树枝器身的形态，造型十分奇特。此槎杯以纯银铸就，细部加以雕刻，槎身半圆，形作枯树，枝桠虬结，树瘿错落，树身中空可盛酒液；一个道士倚树屈膝而坐，长须飘拂，宽袍大袖，手执书卷，神情闲雅，姿态生动。

Silver *Cha* Cup

Cha means the branch of tree. A Cha Cup is a branch-shaped cup with a clever and peculiar ontline. This *Cha* Cup was made of pure silver, with carving in details. The half-round body shaped like a dried-up tree, with the branches and galls mixed up. The cavity of the body can be filled with wine; a Taoist priest with his knees bended, long beard, loose frock and a volume in his hand sits against the tree, who looks elegant and vivid.

- 女金冠

此金冠用极细的竹丝编结而成，并用藤或竹条制成边圈，再在冠壳表面蒙上麻及薄绢。薄绢上用九根金丝箍牢，两侧的金丝弯曲成回旋状。冠的前沿缀有5块镶金边的玉饰。

Gold Crown for Females

This gold crown is made of hairline bamboo thread. The rim is made of vine or bamboo splint, and covered flax and thin silk on the surface. The thin silk is fixed with nine gold threads, and the gold wire on both side is convolutedly bended. The front rim of the crown is embellished five jade decorations with gilding edges.

致，意在追求朴质无华、平淡自然的情趣意味，反对矫揉造作的富丽繁缛之风。此外，宋代金银器的装饰题材也空前丰富，洋溢着淳郁的生活气息。

由于宋代城市的繁荣和商品经济的发展，各地金银器制作行业达到了前所未有的盛况。不少店铺为参与市场竞争和维护商品的信誉，

of the gold and silver articles emerged. Though the articles of this period were less enterprising than that in the Tang Dynasty, the flavor enlightened. Compare to the articles made in the Tang Dynasty, gold and silver articles in the Song Dynasty were more exquisite and fresh, which pursued simple and natural artistic conception, object to the mincing and luxurious style. In addition,

- **银洗和银钵**
  Silver *Xi* (Basin) and Silver *Bo* (Bowl)

- **鎏金银带銙、银梳子**
  銙是古代附于腰带上的装饰品，多用贵重金属制成。
  Gilding Silver Belt *Kua* (Belt Ornament) and Silver Comb
  Kua is an ornament attached on belt used by ancient males, usually made of precious metal.

还把金银店铺和工匠名号以及表明银子成色的印记，都刻印在自己制造的金银器上，有铭款的金银器增多。其中，银器上出现的标明成色的记录，如"吉家煎银十分""周家十分"等，是宋代金银器的一大特点。

元代金银器在吸收宋代金银器特点的基础之上，于形制和品种都有了新的发展，并形成了比较明显的时代风格。从总体上看，元代金银器与宋代相近，但元代某些金银器亦表现出一种纹饰华丽繁复的趋向。这种趋向，对明代以后金银器风格的转变，有着非常重要的影响。

the decoration theme of the gold and silver articles in the Song Dynasty was unprecedentedly rich, full of vitality.

Due to the development of the feudal cities and commodity economy in the Song Dynasty, the gold and silver production workshops could be found anywhere. Many shops sealed the shop and craftsman's name together with the percentage of silver on the products they made. There were more and more gold and silver articles with seal marks. The mark of percentage of silver appeared on silver wares Like "Ji's silver 100 percent", "Zhou's 100 percent", which was one of the characteristics of the gold and silver articles of Song Dynasty.

宋元时期，辽、金、西夏的金银器具有本民族特色，充满了浓厚的异域风情，并与中原金银器风格相互影响，使金银器工艺更加异彩纷呈。

- 鎏金双凤纹银方盒
  Gilding Silver Square Box with Double Phoenix Pattern

- 鎏金花鸟纹提梁铜熏炉
  Gilding Bronze Burner with Flower and Bird Pattern

The gold and silver articles from the Yuan Dynasty (1206-1368) absorbed the characteristics of the Song Dynasty, and further more had new development in appearance and variety, and formed obvious time style. Generally speaking, the gold and silver articles of the Yuan Dynasty were similar with that from the Song Dynasty, but some of them also displayed a tendency of luxuriant complex pattern, which significantly influenced the change in style after the Ming Dynasty (1368-1644).

The gold and silver articles of the Liao, Jin and Western Xia dynasties had strong ethnic characteristics and inter-influenced with the Central Plains' ware style, which contributed to the diversification of the gold and silver article workmanship.

《马可·波罗游记》与元代金银器

元代,意大利人马可·波罗来到中国,并在中国居住了三十多年。在他的著作《马可·波罗游记》中,有许多关于元代金银器的记载,尤其是对金银符牌的记录非常详细。符牌是中国古代朝廷传达命令、征调兵将以及用于处理各项事务的凭证,双方各执一半,合起来以验真伪。

The Travels of Marco Polo and Gold Silver Articles of the Yuan Dynasty

Marco Polo, the Italian came, to China during the Yuan Dynasty, and lived more than thirty years here. In his book *The Travels of Marco Polo*, there are lots of descriptions about gold and silver articles of the Yuan Dynasty, especially the gold or silver tally. A tally consists of two pieces and was used by an emperor for delegating his general with the power to command and dispatch the army, or other affairs. Only when the right half of the tally formed an exact fit with the left, the tally is authenticated as the authorization.

- 柿形银水盂
  Persimmon-shaped Silver Water Calix

- 八棱镀金团花银盒
  Octagonal Gilding Silver Box with Posy Design

明清金银器

明清时期，金银器的制作得到了空前的发展，其技艺集前朝之大成，达到了前所未有的精美、娴熟的程度。其风格以华丽、浓艳的宫廷气息取代了原来的丰满富丽、清秀典雅的特色。尤其是供明清王朝宫廷所用的金银重器，器形和纹样等都呈现出雍容华贵的面貌。龙凤图案象征着不可企及的高贵与权势，这与明清两代宫廷装饰艺术的总体风格相一致。

明代的金银器仍未脱尽宋元时期的古朴风格；而清代金银器一反常态，极为工整华丽。清代皇家所

Gold and Silver Articles of the Ming and Qing Dynasties

The production craft of the gold and silver articles in Ming and Qing dynasties had been developed significantly. Its craft inheriting all the dynasties' achievements was the best ever. Gorgeous and bright-colored royal style displaced the former well-rounded, fine and elegant style. Especially the gold and silver articles provided to the royal courts of the Ming and Qing dynasties, whose appearance and pattern were so dignified and graceful. The countless dragon and phoenix patterns stand for the nobleness and power far beyond people's reach, which were consistent with the overall

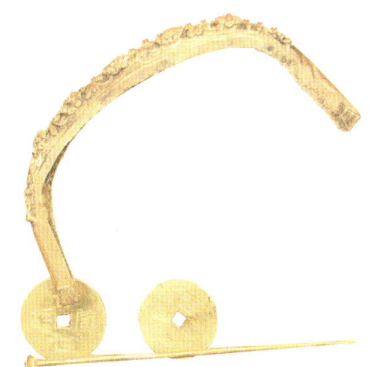

- **金耳扒**
耳扒，即耳挖，是古人用来挖耳朵的器具。
Gold *Erpa* (Ear Pick)
Erpa is a tool of ear cleaning.

- **鎏金银盖罐**
Gilding Silver Pot with Lid

- 金香囊

香囊是古人用来盛香料的小囊，有时也用于避邪除灾，佩挂腰间。此件金香囊为鸡心形，用两片金叶捶压合成，中心微鼓，边缘较薄。

Portable Gold Incense Sachet

The ancients wore sachets at waist to exorcising evil spirits. This heart-shaped sachet is made of two pieces of gold leaves; the center mildly bulges with thin rim.

- 仿雕漆金碗

此碗内施金彩，外饰仿雕漆装饰，雕饰细腻精巧。

Lacquerware-styled Gold Bowl

The inner surface of the bowl is gold and outside is decorated with delicate carved lacquerware style pattern.

- 花卉纹金杯

  Gold Cup with Floral Pattern

- 金云鹤纹瓶

  Gold Jar with Cloud and Crane Pattern

用的金银器几乎遍及典章、祭祀、陈设、佛事、日常生活等诸多方面。与以往历代金银器相比，清代金银器是拥有者和使用者豪华生活的点缀和标志，因此趋向大型化方向发展。在工艺技巧上，清代金银器那种细腻精工，也是明代难以企及的。清代金银工艺的繁荣，不仅继承了中国传统工艺技法，而且有所发展，为现代金银工艺的发展创新奠定了坚实的基础。

● 金镶珠宝帽顶

此帽饰呈三角形，镂饰缠枝花纹，并嵌有红宝石和茶晶。此帽饰造型新颖，精美绝伦，艺术价值极高。

Gold Crown Top Inlaid with Jewels

This hat decoration is in triangle, hollowed out with branches pattern, and inset with rubies and citrines. It is exquisite beyond compare and the artistic value is extremely high.

style of the palace decoration art of the Ming and Qing dynasties.

Gold and silver articles of the Ming Dynasty still remain some natural style from the Song and Yuan dynasties. But the ones of Qing Dynasty are unusually neatly luxuriant. The imperial family of the Qing Dynasty took the use of the gold and silver articles into almost everywhere, including institutions, sacrifice, displays, Buddhist ceremonies, daily life and so on. Compare to the past, the gold and silver articles in the Qing Dynasty were the ornaments and symbol of the owners and users' luxurious life. As a result of that, articles became bigger and bigger. Speaking to the workmanship, the gold and silver articles in the Qing Dynasty were far more delicate than the ones in the Ming Dynasty. The flourishing of the gold and silver craft in the Qing Dynasty not only inherited and developed China's traditional workmanship, but also laid a solid foundation for the development and innovation of the modern gold and silver crafts.

天朝绝响——金编钟

　　编钟是中国古代的一种打击乐器,大多用青铜铸成,由大小不同的扁圆钟按照音调高低的次序排列并悬挂在钟架上,用木槌和棒分别敲击,便能演奏出悦耳的乐曲。清代乾隆皇帝命人以黄金铸造了一套编钟,共耗用黄金一万一千四百两。金编钟是清宫重大典礼时才使用的乐器,是象征皇权的贵重黄金礼器。由于每件器壁的厚薄程度不同,用槌敲击,可以产生不同的音调。按清代制度,每逢有重要典礼的日子,皇帝要亲临太和殿,殿下檐前须设中和韶乐。当皇帝入殿升座、降座离殿时,奏响此乐。这套分两层悬挂于钟架上的金编钟,便是演奏中和韶乐的重要组成部分。

● 天朝绝响——金编钟（图片提供：全景正片）
这套编钟外形略呈椭圆形,腰径外鼓,交龙纽,钟体表面饰有浮雕状的游龙戏珠图案。
The Sound from Heaven of the Imperial Court-Gold Chime-bells
This bell set is shaped like a barrel, with bulgy waist and cross-dragon knob. Each bell is decorated with two dragons sporting with a ball and the patterns of clouds and waves.

The Sound from Heaven of the Imperial Court-Gold Chime-bells

Chime-bells, mostly made of bronze in ancient times, are musical instruments composed with different sized oval-shaped bells hang on to the bell-cot in the order of pitch from high to low and played with mallet. Emperor Qianlong of the Qing Dynasty ordered to make a set of gold chime-bells, which used 11,400 *Liang* (more than 500 kilogram) gold. The Gold Chime-bells were usually played when rites were performed at the royal ancestral or at major ceremonies during Qing Dynasty, symbolizing the imperial power. The bells are in different size and thickness, so they sound different tones. According to the rules of the Qing Dynasty, whenever emperor was sitting down and leave throne in *Taihe* Palace at important ceremonies, the royal music should be played in front of the palace. These hung in two rows on a frame Gold Chime-bells are the major musical instrument to play the music.

清代银饰

清代，各种工艺品都以华丽为尚，手工艺的水平也达到了登峰造极的程度，金银器的雕刻、镂空、花丝、珐琅等获得了较大的发展。康熙、乾隆年间，银器、银饰品的使用不再是贵族阶层的专利，而是步入了普通家庭，女人头戴银头饰、男人腰佩银挂件已成为一种时尚。银楼、银作坊、银店分布全国各地，做工也越来越讲究，银饰品在民间大放异彩。清代银饰的种类很多，主要有簪、钗、步摇、扁方、帽花、长命锁等。

Silver Accessories of the Qing Dynasty

All art articles feature in magnificence in the Qing Dynasty (1616-1911). The workmanship had reached its peak. The gold and silver articles' carving, hollowing, filigree and enamel skills were well developed. During the reign of Emperor Kangxi and Qianlong, the usage of silver articles was not limited to the nobles anymore. Women wearing silver head wear and men hanging silver pendants in their waists had become fashion of that time. Silver shops and silver workshops could be found all over the country. The craft was more and more delicate. There were a variety of silver accessories in the Qing Dynasty, mainly including *Zan* (hairpin), *Chai* (hairpin), *Buyao* (shaking-while-walking hairpin), *Bianfang*, hat ornament, Longevity Lock, and so on.

• 银梳子

梳子是一种梳理头发用的工具，由上往下梳，有凡事疏通之意。

Silver Comb

Comb is used to put hairs in order, from top to bottom, symbolizing that everything goes unobstructed.

• 银手镯

银手镯是古代民间花样最丰富、佩戴人群最多的首饰，也是一种吉祥物，是姑娘出嫁时最起码的订婚礼物。

Silver Bracelet

Silver bracelet was the most popular ornaments with the richest styles in ancient times. It was also a symbol of good luck, and was an elementary gift for engagement.

• 银步摇

步摇是簪首有坠件的饰品，造型多种多样，多有珠花下垂，女人戴在头上走起路来则会摇动，故名。

Silver Shaking-while-walking Hairpins (*Buyao*)

Buyao was hairpin of filigree worn by women in ancient China which has heads shaped in many styles, usually with colorful pearls and small jade additions, which were loosely made so as to sway when the wearer moves. That's how the name comes.

• 银长命锁

长命锁是明清时期挂在孩童脖子上的一种装饰物，取"锁住生命"之意，形状多样，多刻有吉祥文字和图案。

Silver Longevity Lock

The longevity lock was an ornament hanging on child's neck during the Ming and Qing dynasties, symbolizing that life is as safe as being locked in a safe box. With multiple shapes, it was mostly carved with auspicious characters and patterns.

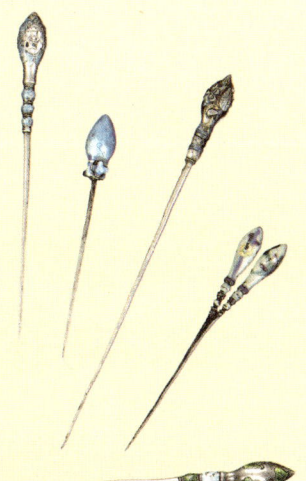

• 银点蓝头簪

簪钗是一种发间饰品，插入发内的细长部分称为"挺"，单挺为簪，双挺以上为钗。

Silver Hairpin with Dotted Blue Pattern

Two kinds of hairpins were used very often in ancient times. The one pin style is called *Zan* in Chinese and the two-pin-fork style is called *Chai*.

• 银帽花

帽花是指装饰在帽子上或额间的饰品，多用于小孩出生过满月、百天、周岁等喜庆节日，一般以神仙、花卉、八宝等吉祥物为主。

Silver Hat Ornaments

Hat ornaments are worn on hats or foreheads on children's first month or the 100th day of birth or the first birthday to celebrate new life. They are usually with auspicious patterns such as immortals, flowers, or eight treasures.

• 银扁方

扁方是满族妇女特有的头饰，满族妇女有一种特殊的发饰名为"两把头"，扁方是用来固定这种发饰的饰物。扁方扁平，呈"一"字型，浑朴而大方。

Silver *Bianfang*

Bianfang is an exclusive specialized headwear for women from Man ethnic group, who had a special hairstyle named *Liangbatou*, and *Bianfang* is a headwear to fix that hairstyle. *Bianfangs* are horizontal flats, simple and elegant.

清代宫廷金银器的等级

清代宫殿、寝室里陈设的金银器比比皆是，涵盖了餐饮、起居、娱乐休闲等宫廷生活的方方面面。为了体现皇族的尊贵，清廷还从数量、成色等方面对金银器的使用做了严格的规定。据文献记载，皇帝的膳房设有"金锅三件，金碗十一件……银锅十五件，银大盘一百三十件……银碗二十五件，银碟二百三十件。"皇后及嫔妃们使用的金银器的数量随品级的降低而减少。

The Grade of Gold and Silver Articles Used in Royal Court of the Qing Dynasty

Gold and silver articles could be seen everywhere in the royal palaces of the Qing Dynasty (1616-1911), covered all the aspects including catering, daily life, entertainment and so on. To embody the dignity of the imperial family, the royal court had strict rules referred to the quantity and quality of the gold and silver articles. According to the literature records, the kitchen of the emperor was equipped with "3 gold pans, 11 gold bowls…15 silver pans, 130 giant silver plates…25 silver bowls, 230 silver plates." The gold and silver articles' quantity of the queen and imperial concubines reduced by their estates.

- 金凤冠

此凤冠框由金丝编成，上面缀云彩，并有五凤四凰，中心一朵大牡丹；圆形火焰字牌八个，各阴刻楷书一字，另有长方形火焰牌一块上阴刻"恩荣"二字；抹额为双龙戏珠纹。

Gold Phoenix Coronet

The frame is woven with gold wire, embellished with cloud, peony, five *Feng* and four *Huang* (nine phoenixes). Eight round frame-shaped plates are with one regular script character carved on each, and one rectangle frame plate carved with two characters meaning "grace". The pattern of double dragons playing bead is on the forehead.

- 金镂空古钱纹镯

此镂空古钱纹镯为清代后妃佩戴的首饰，是以细金丝条捶击成一个古钱形并将其连接成镯，首尾结合处几乎天衣无缝。虽光素无纹饰，但由一个个金钱形组合成的镂空钱纹镯，在清代后妃所佩戴的诸多首饰中实属罕见。

Gold Bracelet with Hollow Ancient Coins Pattern

This bracelet was for the queen and concubines of the Qing Dynasty, made of thin gold wire hammered into coin-shape and connected together. The joint points are perfect. Though with no pattern, a coin-shaped hollow bracelet could be rarely seen among the accessories of the queen and concubines' at that time.

- 铜镀金掐丝珐琅熏炉

Copper Gilding Filigree Enamel Burner

金银器的工艺
The Craft of the Gold and Silver Articles

　　在古代，金银器属于一种贵族消费品，制造过程中往往不计工本，以展现王室贵族的审美趣味和高贵身份，因而在工艺上达到了很高的造诣。中国古代金银器不仅类型多样，范围广泛，而且工艺极其复杂精细。一件精美绝伦的金银器，从锻造到装饰加工，一般需要使用多种工艺。

In ancient times, the gold and silver articles were consumed by the nobility, who spared no expense to show their taste and dignity. That made the craft reach very high attainments. The gold and silver articles from the ancient China were various in kind, wide in scale and complex in craft. To make a fine article, many techniques are needed from forging to decoration.

> 锻造技术

金银器的品类不同，其制作工艺也各不相同。一般说来，金银器的锻造技术就是以金银为原料，进行制胎、浇铸、锻打、焊接、烧制、打磨、冲压、电镀等程序。通过了解这些复杂的锻造工艺，就可以感受到中国的古代先民们所拥有的无限的智慧。

范铸

范铸是中国最早的金器加工方法之一。它仿照青铜铸造工艺，先按所要制作的器形制模翻范，然后把金矿石或自然金石加热至1063℃，熔化成金液，再浇入预先准备好的器物模范内，冷却后即成所要制作的器物。银器范铸的程序也相同，但熔化温度要降至

> Forging Technology

Different types of gold and silver wares are made by different skills. Generally speaking, the forging technology of gold and silver articles include smelting, mould founding, hammering, welding, casting, firing, polishing, punching, electro facing etc. Knowing these complex forging technologies, one can feel the infinite wisdom of the Chinese ancient ancestors.

Model Founding

Model Founding is one of the earliest methods for processing gold and silver articles in China, originated from bronze making. The gold ores or natural gold stones are heated to 1063℃ and the liquid gold is filled into models to get articles designed after cooling. The process of silver articles making is the same, beside of the melting temperature low down

- **鎏金铜钫**

钫是一种酒器，此铜钫通体鎏金，腹上部两侧有对称的铺首衔环。

Gilding Bronze *Fang*

Fang is a kind of wine vessel. This all-over gilded bronze *Fang* has a pair of animal head bear rings on both sides of the upper belly.

- **错金银鸟纹虎子**

虎子是古代一种便器。此虎子造型扁圆，大腹，管状流，通体饰金银丝镶嵌纹饰，腹部以鸟纹为主题纹饰，口部、腹下部饰V形连纹，器底部饰涡纹。

Gold Inlayed Silver *Huzi* with Bird Pattern

Huzi is the jordan in ancient times. This one shaped oblate and has a giant belly. The body was inset with patterns of gold and silver wire, a bird theme pattern on the belly, V-shaped pattern on the mouth and the under part of the belly, and vortex pattern on the bottom.

960.8℃。由于范铸技术很难制出薄胎器物，因此胎体厚重就成了范铸器物的主要特点。锤鍱技术普遍应用后，范铸方法就很少采用了。

锤鍱

锤鍱是绝大多数金属器物成型前必须经过的锻造工艺。其方法是先锤打金银板片，使之逐渐延伸展

to 960.8℃. This molding technique can hardly produce thin and light articles, so thick and heavy is the major feature of model founding articles, which is barely used after the hammering technique being widespread.

Hammering

The hammering technique is the necessary forging process for most metal

颈：颈部饰两道宽厚弦纹，两侧为缠枝状立耳。

Neck: Two wide and thick bowstring patterns are craved on the neck and a pair of branch-shaped prick ears are added on the both sides of the neck.

壶身：壶身正、背两面开光，内錾刻双夔龙戏缠枝莲花图案，呈浮雕状。

Body: There is an open frame on each side of the body, carved with relief pattern of double dragons playing in branches and lotus.

回纹：壶体两侧、壶颈和底足均刻满整齐的回纹。

Rectangular Spirals Pattern: Both sides of body, neck and base are full of carved rectangular spirals pattern.

- 金錾花扁壶

此壶壶体呈扁圆形，圆口，直颈，颈较短粗，底足作梯形。此壶造型典雅，花纹雅致、缜密，且又十分规整，精雕细琢，堪为清宫中一件极精美的工艺品，是錾雕工艺的杰作。

Gold Flat Flask with Carved Patterns

The flask has an oblate shape, round month, straight neck that is short and thick, and a ladder-shaped base foot. This pot has an elegance appearance and delicate pattern, sure to be a masterpiece from the Qing's palace.

- 赤金盆

Pure Gold Pot

- 狮纽牡丹金银香薰
Gold and Silver Incense Burner with Lion Knob and Peony Pattern

of the articles. The process of hammering is to firstly thump the gold and silver sheets into pieces, then place the pieces of gold and silver into the matrix and hammer to various shapes. This method can be also used to make decoration patterns. Some simple shaped articles can be produced by hammering for just one time, while the complex shaped articles should be hammered in different parts separately and then weld together. The hammering technique costs less material and less workers than the molding method, so it is very popular to be used in the articles which use soft and precious materials like gold and silver. Most of the Tang Dynasty's (618-907) gold and silver utensils like the bowls and plates were made by hammering technique.

Casting

The casting process is a precise investment casting craft. The specific process is firstly to make a wax body in fusible wax or other fusible materials, then pour the body with fine mud for times to form a mud shell, fix up the internal and external molds and casting system, and paint it with fireproofing for the hardening; after the drying, heat

开成片状，再将片状金银置于模具之中打成各种器形，也可用这种方法制作装饰花纹。一些形体简单、较浅的器物可以一次直接锤制出来，而复杂的器物则先分别锤制出各个部分，然后焊接在一起。用锤鍱法制造的器物要比铸造耗用的材料少，也不像范铸器物时需要多人分工合作，所以该法在质地较软又十分珍贵的金银器物制作中极为盛行。唐代金银器皿中的大多数碗、盘、碟等都是用锤鍱术制作的。

浇铸

浇铸是一种精密的熔模铸造技术。其具体做法是，先用易熔的蜡或其他易熔材料熔化制成蜡胎，然后用细泥浆多次浇淋，形成泥料外形，做上内模和外模，装上浇注系统，并涂上耐火材料使之硬化；阴干后，加热使蜡胎熔化流出，再入窑焙烧；烧成后，形成有空腔的铸型，四周用砂填实，便可浇铸金液或银液，铸造复杂的金银器。在做铸型（里、外模）时，不需起模，铸型无分型面，型腔厚薄均匀，铸件壁厚可小至0.3毫米以下，铸件的形状很少受限制，表面具有一定光洁度，能在金银器中精确再现细微变化。

浇铸工艺的最大特点是，使用可熔模料代替不可熔模料作模，因此在古代多用于铸造具有复杂形制的铸件。

it till the wax melts and flows out and then put into the kiln and roast; after the roasting, a mould with cavity is formed and surrounded with sand, which can be poured with liquid gold or silver and cast complex gold and silver articles. There is no need for the drawing when making the mould, the mould has no molded surfaces, the thickness is even and can be controlled below 0.3 mm. The shape of the mould has no limit, the surface of which can be glabrous, and can display detailed patterns on the gold and silver articles.

The most obvious feature of the casting process is placing the infusible materials with fusible one when making the mould, thus it was mostly used to cast the foundries with complex shapes in ancient times.

• 金胎烧铸珐琅玉柄佩刀
Gold Base Casting Enamel Sabre with Jade Handle

古代的银楼

银楼是指中国古代生产金银首饰器皿并从事交易的商店。从唐代开始，民间就已建有银楼。到了清代，银楼的数量更多，比如上海的九大银楼（凤祥裕记、杨庆和、裘天宝等），以制造锁、镯、簪、戒指、压发等女式金银饰品为主。民国初期，由于人们接受了西方饰品的风格，传统的金银饰品产量减少，于是各大银楼逐渐开始制造金银器皿等日用品。

Silver Shops in Ancient Times

The silver shops were the shops producing and trading gold and silver articles in ancient China. The silver shops emerged in folk since the Tang Dynasty. By the time of the Qing Dynasty, a greater number of these shops appeared, like the nine biggest silver shops in Shanghai (The *Fengxiang Yuji*, the *Yang Qinghe*, *Qiu Tianbao*, etc.), which mainly produced gold and silver accessories for women like locks, bracelets, headwears, rings and so on. In the early Minguo Period, as people accepted the western style, the production volume of the traditional gold and silver accessories reduced, and these silver shops gradually began to produce articles for daily use like gold and silver utensils.

- 金双凤链牌
Gold Chain Plate with Double Phoenixes Pattern

- 银耳坠
Silver Eardrops

焊接与铆接

　　焊接是中国古代金银器制作的传统工艺之一。所谓的焊接就是把器物的部件以及纹饰同器体连接成整体的一种工艺。其具体方法是通过加热使得焊药熔化，将被焊部件与主体粘结牢固。焊药的主要成分一般与被焊物相同，加少量硼砂混合而成，也有用银与铜为主料合成的焊药。焊接后需对焊痕进行处理，如果焊技高超，那么在器物上几乎看不出焊接的痕迹。

　　古代金银器的连接工艺除了焊接外，还有铆接。所谓的铆接就是将接件和主体间凿出小孔，用穿钉钉牢，主要用于器把、提梁等部件的连接。

Welding and Riveting

The welding was one of the earliest traditional gold and silver producing crafts in ancient China. So called welding is a process to connect the parts and patterns of the articles to the main body. The specific process is firstly to melt the welding agent by heating, and then firmly attach the welded part to the main body. The main material of the welding agent usually is the same as the welded part mixed with a small quantity of borax. Sometimes the welding agent can be composed by copper and silver; after the welding the weld marks have to be concealed, and no mark can be found when it comes to an excellent welding craftsman.

　　The riveting was another jointing process in ancient times. So called riveting is to pick a small hole between the union piece

● 金壶
Gold Pot

退火与酸洗

退火又叫"淬火",是金银器加工过程中比较重要的工艺之一。金、银等金属加工原料在加工之前都应退火,退火后的金、银原料变得柔软,加工起来相对比较容易一些,而且不易碎裂。退火就是先用火烧烤金片或银片,直到将其烘烤至完全发红,并维持一段时间,然后用酸液浸泡,再用清水冲洗干净。

and the main body and nail them down with drift bolt. This craft was mainly used in the jointing of parts like handles or straps.

Annealing and Pickling

Annealing is one of the major crafts of the processing of the gold and silver articles. Metal materials like gold and silver should all be annealed before the processing to make them soft and unbreakable, and easier to be processed. The process of the annealing is to firstly

- 银质佛龛

Silver Shrine of the Buddha

- 鎏金珐琅盅

盅是古人饮酒或喝茶用的没有把儿的杯子。此盅通体施浅蓝色珐琅釉,内施黄铜镀金,外壁纹饰中有四个圆形开光,分别饰有"万""寿""无""疆"四个篆字。

Gilding Enamel *Zhong*

Zhong is the cup without handle used by the ancients to drink tea or wine. This *Zhong* is glazed with light blue enamel on gilded copper base. Outside surface is decorated with four round clear opening Chinese characters in seal scripts, which means "Boundless Longevity".

一些金银器工件加热后因氧化会变黑，于是古人将工件在仍然热的时候放入酸液中浸泡除去黑色氧化物，这就是酸洗。

打磨与抛光

打磨的目的是让金银器表面比较光滑，没有杂质。其具体做法是先用莝草（一种长有毛刺的草，相当于现在的砂纸）或磨石打磨，直到用肉眼看不到明显的锉痕为止。古人有时会用木条裹住莝草打磨，木条可以是圆形的也可以是方形的，木条根据需要可大可小。裹在木条上的莝草根据工序变动可以变

burn the gold or silver pieces in fire till they completely turn red. Then wait for a minute and wash them with acid liquor. After that clean them up in branch water.

Some gold and silver parts would turn black after the heating for the oxidizing reaction. Soaking these parts into the acid liquor when they were still in heat can detach the black oxide, which is called the pickling.

Grinding and Polishing

The goal of the grinding is to make the surface of the articles smooth and wipe off the impurities. The detail process is to firstly use the file grass (a kind of grass with burr, like the modern abrasive paper) or millstone to rub till there is no visible file mark at all. Sometimes the ancients use stick covered with the file grass for the rubbing, which could be round or square and big or small according to the need. The file grass covering on the stick could be adjusted according to the changes of the process. A well-done grinding job can improve the speed and quality of the polishing work later.

Polishing means to remove the coarse part on the surface of the articles by cutting, rasping, wiping and so on to

• 抛光金提梁罐
Polished Gold Jar with Loop Hand

银双喜圆形粉盒
Silver Round Powder Box with Double Happiness Pattern

换。只有打磨工作做好了，最后的抛光工艺才能既省事又光亮。

　　所谓的抛光，就是指用切削、锉磨、擦拭等方法除去器物表面的毛糙部分，使器物显得平圆光滑。通常经过抛光的金银器十分光亮、华丽无比。古代的抛光操作比较简单，用一根约三十厘米长，约二三厘米粗细的木条粘上小山羊皮制成抛光棍；在山羊皮上抹些抛光剂，摩擦金银器就可以抛光了。首饰有些难以用抛光棍抛光的地方，就需要用抛光线来抛光。先将抛光线用油浸泡后，将其挂在架子上，然后将抛光剂涂抹在抛光线上，再用手拽住线头进行抛光。

smooth the articles. Generally a polished gold or silver article can be very notable and gorgeous. The polishing process in ancient times was simple, having a stick of 30 centimeters long and about 2 to 3 centimeters thick attached with a piece of goat fur to be the polishing stick. After mopped some polishing agent on goat fur the stick can be used for the polishing by rubbing the gold or silver wears. Some parts of the accessories are hard to polish by the stick, and then the polishing wire is needed. Firstly soak the wire in oil. Then hang it up on a shelf and paint the polishing agent on the wire. At last hold the wire with hands to do the polishing.

金银器的年代鉴定
Age Identification of Gold and Silver Articles

　　金银器制造年代的鉴别十分困难和复杂，只能依靠经验的积累。一般来说，金银器制造年代的鉴别可从铭文、造型、纹饰、制造工艺等方面的综合分析进行间接的推断。

To identify ages of gold and silver articles is very difficult and complex. The only tool can be relied on is experience. Generally speaking, comprehensive analysis of the inscription, shape, pattern and craft can indirectly infer the age of a gold or silver articles.

铭文 Inscription

　　器物上的铭文款识是最直接、最准确的断代依据。铭文款识可以在内容、书法、行文规矩等几个方面给予断代信息。从中国金银器的发展看，唐代以前金银器上的铭文很少见；宋元以后，有铭文款识的金银器明显多了起来。有些金银器上虽然没有铭文，但也可以通过同地出土的其他形制相近的金银器上的铭文，间接进行年代推断。

　　The inscriptions on the articles are the most direct and precise evidence of age. Information of the age can be found from aspects including the content, penmanship, style or manner of writing of the inscriptions. In the development of China's gold and silver articles, the ones before the Tang Dynasty almost had no inscription at all; the inscription became normal after the Song and Yuan dynasties. Some articles have no inscription, but one can check the inscriptions on the similar articles excavated from the same place to judge its age indirectly.

造型 Shape

　　金银器的制作离不开社会的文化背景，每件器物都不免打上时代的烙印，这也是判断时代的依据。根据造型来推断年代，首先要把握其整体气息，熟悉各个时代金银器的风格，比如器皿中的杯、碗、盆等，在魏晋南北朝时期是什么造型，到了唐宋时期又是什么造型，尤其要注意的是只为某个时代所特有的造型或形制。其次是要把握各种造

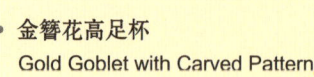

• 金錾花高足杯
Gold Goblet with Carved Pattern

- **摩羯纹金羽觞**

  摩羯是印度神话中一种长鼻利齿、鱼身鱼尾的神异动物，被尊奉为河水之精、生命之本，常见于古代印度的雕塑和绘画艺术中。东晋时期，随着佛经的汉译，摩羯被介绍到了中国；唐代之后，它成了金银器中较为常见的装饰图案。

  Gold *Shang* (Wine Vessel) with Makara Pattern

  Makara is a mythical creature with long nose, sharp teeth, fish body and tail in the Hindu mythology, accepted as the spirit of the river and the essence of life, which can be seen in the Ancient India's sculptures and art of paintings. During the Eastern Jin Dynasty (317-420), the Makara was introduced to China together with the recommended of the Buddhist sutras; since the Tang Dynasty, it became a regular pattern on the gold and silver articles.

型出现直至消失的时间，即器物存在的时空范围。比如有着比较明显的外来风格的高足杯、带把杯主要流行于魏晋至唐代中前期，以后则很少出现。

    The producing of the gold and silver articles couldn't be separated from their social culture background; every article would naturally have some features of that time, which can be used to judge its age. Inferring the age by the shapes, one should firstly master the styles of each period, like what the shapes of articles in the same variety should be look like in different dynasties, especially should notice the particular shapes which belongs to a particular period. Secondly one should master the emerging and disappearing time of each shape, which is the coverage of the ware. For example, the goblets and handled cups which had obvious foreign style were mainly used from the Wei and Jin dynasties to the mid-term of the Tang Dynasty, later of that which barely can be seen.

纹饰 Pattern

    纹饰代表各个历史时期人们的审美情趣和文化素养，是比较敏感、易于变化的器物特征之一，因此也是判断器物制造年代的一个重要因素。依据纹饰判断年代，主要应掌握三点内容。

    （1）各个时期或地区所特有的某种纹饰。如摩羯纹只见于唐代而其他时代均不曾出现过，以动物纹为主体纹饰的各种金牌饰只出现在战国至两汉时期的北方少数民族地区。

（2）同一纹饰在不同时期的特点。龙凤是中国古代使用最多的一种纹样，但各个时期的龙凤纹样也有着明显的区别。如唐代的龙，一般是单个出现，三爪，形象较为朴实，而明代的龙，多成对出现，五爪，极富神异色彩；唐代的凤，有的像长尾鸟，有的像孔雀，与飞禽悬殊不大，而明代的凤身体蜷曲，形象凶狠。

（3）参考其他质地器物上的纹饰。同一时期不同质地的各类器物，由于受特定时代氛围的限制，在装饰题材上往往表现出相似或相同的特点。据此，在利用纹饰判断制造时代时，应尽可能多参考其他质地的文物。

The pattern stands for the appreciation of the beauty and cultural literacy of the people in different periods. It is one of the sensitive and changeful characteristics of those articles, thus is also an important factor to judge the age of the articles. Judging age by patterns, there are three aspects should be noticed.

(1) Specific patterns of each period or area. Like the makara pattern only appeared in the Tang Dynasty, and the gold plates and accessories with animals as the main pattern only appeared in the northern ethnic minority areas from the Warring States Period to the Han Dynasty.

(2) The characteristics of the same pattern in different periods. The dragon and phoenix were the mostly used pattern in ancient

- 光绪款金执壶
Gold Ewer Made in Emperor Guangxu's Reign

China, but these patterns in different period had obvious differences. For example, the dragon pattern from the Tang Dynasty usually appeared single with three claws and simple shape, while the dragon pattern from the Ming Dynasty mostly is in pairs with five claws and a riot of colors; the phoenix of the Tang Dynasty looks like reedling or peacock which is similar to the regular bird, the ones from the Ming Dynasty appeared twisted and fierce.

(3) The patterns of the articles made of other materials. As the articles of the same time but different materials are limited to the atmosphere at specific time, usually possess the same or similar decoration features. For this reason, when judging the age by the patterns, one should refer to the other articles with different materials as more as possible.

制造工艺 Craft

制造工艺在一定程度上也能反映出各个时代的特征。中国古代金银工艺，从商周至明清，每一时代都在继承前代的基础上不断推陈出新并由此形成各自的时代工艺特征。如银器的夹层做法，宋代以前没有发现，但在宋代却较为常见；再如点烧透明珐琅工艺在清朝才出现。

The crafts can reflect the features of different periods to a certain degree. The ancient China's gold and silver crafts from the Shang and Zhou dynasties to the Ming and Qing dynasties are step by step formed specific technological characteristics of each period. For example, the interlayer skill of the silver articles didn't show up until the Song Dynasty, and no article make with spot welding transparent enamel craft was found before the Qing Dynasty.

• 金錾花执壶

此壶是清代皇帝的御用酒具，呈葫芦形，盖上饰花蕾形纽，器身上以錾刻和镂雕的技法雕刻云龙纹。

Gold Ewer with Carved Patterns

This wine pot was of exclusive use for the emperor at grand banquets at the court in the Qing Dynasty. In shape of calabash with carved and hollowed cloud and dragon patterns on the body, the lid is decorated with bud-shaped knob.

> 装饰工艺

一件件传世的巧夺天工的金银器，是中国古代金银器装饰工艺的完美体现。古代的装饰工艺包括鎏金、贴金、包金、錾刻、模冲、累丝、错金银、金银平脱、炸珠、点蓝等。

鎏金

鎏金工艺早在战国时期就已经出现，到了汉代，鎏金技术发展到了很高的水平，唐代时期大量运用于银器装饰。中国古代鎏金技术

> Decoration Craft

The immortal and supernatural gold and silver articles perfectly embody the decoration craft of the ancients. The ancient decoration craft includes gilding, gold pasting, gold cladding, carving, filigree work, gold inlaying, gold and silver cutting, gold beading, enameling and so on.

Gilding

The gilding technique has emerged in the Warring States Period (475 B.C.-221 B.C.). By the Han Dynasty (206 B.C.-220 A.D.), it developed to a high level, and was massively used in the silver ware decoration in the Tang Dynasty

• 铜鎏金嵌玉饰
Gilding Copper Ornament Inlaid with Jade

- 鎏金带盖珐琅鼎式炉
  Gilding Enamel *Ding* (Cauldron)-style Stove with Cover

多用"泥金法"。文献记载："水银能消化金银使成泥，人以镀物也。"其方法是首先将成色优质的黄金锤成金叶，剪成细丝，放入坩埚中加热烧红，按一两黄金加七两水银的比例加入水银混合成金汞，俗称"金泥"。然后将金泥涂抹在所需鎏金器物的表面，其后在火上烘烤器物。水银遇热蒸发，金留存于器表，鎏金器遂成。如果要加厚鎏金层，可反复进行几次。

鎏金工艺又可分通体鎏金和局部鎏金两种。局部鎏金即只在纹饰部分鎏金，也分两种，一是刻好花纹后再鎏金，二是鎏金后再刻花

(618-907). The major gilding technique in ancient China was called the "Paste Gold Method". The following words recorded in ancient document, "The mercury can digest the gold and silver into paste, with which people plate on bronze". First, hammer the fine gold into gold leaves and cut into filaments, heat them in the crucible to red, and then mix with mercury according to the scale 1:7 to get the gold paste. Second, paint the gold paste on the surface of the object and dry over the fire. The mercury will be evaporated by the heat while the gold remains. This process can be repeated several times to gain thicker layer.

● 银鎏金曼陀罗
"曼陀罗"是藏传佛教用语，指圣贤的聚集之所。
Gilding Silver Mandala
Tibetan Buddhists call the gathering place of the sages Mandala.

There are two kinds of gilding techniques, full gilding and partial gilding. The partial gilding means only the ornamental design part is gilded, which is also divided into two types. One is to gild after carving pattern, the other is to gild before carving. The first method was mainly used in the early Tang Dynasty; the second method was more common in the middle and later period of the Tang Dynasty. Partial gilded articles occupy a large proportion of silver wares of the Tang Dynasty, which were called Gold Flower Silver Wares.

The major feature of the gilding craft is that the gold layer is extremely thin and tight, looking very natural. It's hard to distinguish a delicate fully-gilded article from a pure gold one. The former sometimes is regarded as the latter by mistake.

纹。前者主要流行于唐代前期，后者多见于中晚唐。局部鎏金的器物在唐代银器中占有相当大的比重，文献中称之为"金花银器"。

鎏金工艺的最大的特点是鎏金层极薄，而且紧密，看不出刻意装饰。精致的通体鎏金器与金器很难分辨，有时会被误认为是金器。

Gold Pasting and Gold Cladding

Gold pasting is sticking gold foil on part of an article with varnish gum, or by the roughness of the surface. A fine gold pasting ware can be mistaken for gilded one. This technique was used more than three thousand years ago. Gold also can be pasted on lacquer wares. The major

贴金与包金

贴金，是用胶漆之类的黏合剂把金片贴于某种器物的装饰部位，或利用器物的凹凸面使之紧贴于器物的表面。处理得较好的贴金常被误认为是鎏金。此工艺最早在商代中期就已经被采用，主要使用于先秦时期。贴于漆器表面的叫"金髹"或"浑金漆"。贴金专用材料主要有金箔、银箔、铜箔、铝箔。

传统贴金装饰方法是将金箔用竹钳子夹起，贴在有黏性的底子上，一般贴于织物、皮革、纸张、各种器物以及建筑物表面作装饰materials of gold pasting are gold, silver, copper and aluminum foil.

The traditional method is picking gold foil with bamboo tong and sticking to the viscous surface of fabric, leather, paper, articles and constructions. The surface where to be pasted should be painted with the vesicae glue, which was the ancient ways in the Tang and Song dynasties. This technique was widespread in the Tang Dynasty (618- 907). In the Song Dynasty (960-1279) gold trade was forbidden due to the shortage. Gold pasting was mainly used for constructive decoration in the Yuan, Ming and Qing dynasties.

● 金漆勾莲团寿碗
Gold Lacquer Bowl with Lotus and Round Longevity Pattern

● 包金龙纹玉腰带片
Gold-clad Jade Belt Pieces with Dragon Pattern

用。贴金的底子，用鱼鳔胶水遍刷一层，这是唐宋的古法。唐代贴金工艺已经非常普遍，宋代时期由于黄金竭乏，素有销金禁令。元、明、清时期，贴金工艺主要用于建筑装饰。

包金是一种既有保护功能又有装饰器物作用的工艺，所包对象一般都是小型器件。所谓的包金，是指在铜器等器物外面包上一层薄金片，这种工艺手法在西周时期已被采用，主要用在金银器不太发达的先秦时期。包金和贴金一样，都属于薄金工艺。

The gold cladding is for decorating and protecting. The objects are small in size. It is to clad the articles like the bronze with a layer of thin gold plate. This technique was first used in the Western Zhou Dynasty and was mainly used before the Qin Dynasty when gold and silver article making was not developed. Like gold pasting, gold wrapping is also a thin gold work.

• 包金法螺
Gold-clad Ritual Conch

金器的保养

　　黄金性质柔软，延展性强，不易受腐蚀，保养起来较为容易。但由于黄金是一种不用加工就具有很高经济价值的贵金属，因此一般金制品中常掺入银、铜或铁的成分，使金变硬，从而改变金的颜色或降低其高昂的价格。比如金片、金箔、鎏金等制品常用合金材料或只是部分用金制成。金和铜混合，通常也夹杂一些银，铸出的铜金器呈淡黄色，甚至呈绿色。但经过多年埋藏后，因土中的盐类清除了合金表面的浅层金属，结果留下一层纯金薄片，淡黄色就会转变成一种熟黄色，其色彩艳丽，具有很高的收藏价值。

　　经过长期使用，纯金制品一般不会有太大的变化，但合金的器物因加工过程中可能形成细小的空隙，当水进入时则会发生腐蚀。鎏金器物也会有肉眼所见不到的裂缝、空隙和微细的孔，水或水汽钻进去可产生电解腐蚀，不断破坏除金以外的其他金属。

　　铜氧化形成绿色的薄锈，可用酸类或氨水去除；表面覆盖红色锈的可用一点盐酸去掉。薄片的金叶饰品可经过按压展平；如果较易折裂，则需适当地加热回火使其软化展平。但对于鎏金的金属器物，则不能采用还原方法来处理，因为这种做法可能损伤鎏金，所以，不妨使用碱性酒石酸钾钠来清除其他金属的锈蚀。

● 金羊虎饰件
Gold Sheep and Tiger Ornament

● 镂空葫芦形金耳环
Hollow Gold Calabash-shaped Cup with Handles

如果其他金属已被锈蚀物所堆盖，而且在这些物质下面或物质中间有一层鎏金的薄层，可采用机械法清除。在显微镜下用钢针挑除锈蚀，当露出鎏金的薄层时，用1%的稀硝酸把鎏金的表面清洗一下，但绝不可用硝酸来软化锈壳，否则将使金饰脱落。

值得注意的是，黄金制品虽很少有因外界因素而受到侵害的，但是一切机械性损害都是很危险的，往往最轻的冲击，用粗糙布片粗率地拂拭，都能致使扭曲、压皱、擦伤，破坏表面的光泽。因此保管金器物品的房屋，必须保持干燥，没有尘埃和空气污染物；温度18~24℃，相对湿度40%~50%。金器应装在锦套、垫棉花的盒子里，件与件之间不能彼此碰撞。不可除去古器物上的薄膜，这是由于氧化作用而形成的一层附加金属，也就是人们常说的包浆。此外，黄金制品与其他金属制品不能一起保存，要用软毛刷除去灰尘，用柔软的羚羊皮拂拭；如果必须清洗，可用乙醚、汽油（苯）、中性肥皂沫或氨水（10%浓度）来进行，然后用蒸馏水洗净、烘干，不可用任何涂剂、质地硬的羚羊皮擦拭。

• 金花簪
Gold Flowery Hairpin

The Maintenance of Gold Articles

Gold is a precious metal treasured for its malleability, softness and resistance to corrosion, which is easy to be maintained. But many gold products are mixed with silver, copper or iron to increase the hardness, change its color or lower the cost. Like gold sheet, gold foil and gilded products are usually made of alloy materials or partially made of gold. The bronzes made of mixed gold and copper, sometimes added silver, display light yellow in color, sometimes even green. But after being buried in the ground for many years, the salt in the soil obliterated the shallow metal in the surface of the alloy and left a thin pure gold layer, turning light yellow into ripe yellow. Such gorgeous color should be retained.

The pure gold products normally don't change after thousands years' erosion. But for the alloy articles as some tiny gaps might be produced during the processing, when water drops in the corrosion would occur. The gilded articles also have some invisible gaps, interspaces and tiny holes. When water or vapors pass through they could generate electrolytic corrosion, which will continuously damage the other metals except for gold.

The green flash rusting caused by the copper oxidation can be removed by acid or ammonia water; the red rust on the surface can be removed with a little of muriatic acid. The thin gold leaf accessories can adopt pressing-to-flat method; if the material is easy to break, it needs to be appropriately heated to soften the metal and then the piece can be flattened. But for the gilding metal articles, reduction method cannot be used, because it would damage the gilding. The solution is to use the alkaline tartaric acid potassium sodium to clean up the rust of the other metals.

If other metals have been covered by the rust, below or within the rust and there is a gilding layer, mechanic method is recommended. That is using steel needle to pick rust under microscope to reveal the gilding layer, and to clean the surface with 1% dilute nitric acid. Remember never use nitric acid to soften the rust shell. It can break off the gold.

It's worth noting that though gold products are barely damaged by the natural factures, all mechanical damages are dangerous. Even the slightest strike or rough and careless whisk by a coarse cloth can cause tortuosity, crumple, and bruising and damage the luster of the surface. Therefore, the room keeping the gold articles must be dry without dust and air pollution, and keep temperature 18-24℃ , relative humidity 40%-50%. The gold articles should be wrapped by cotton-padded bags and kept in cotton-filled boxes, out of clashing. The thin layer added by oxidation on the ancient articles shouldn't be removed. This layer caused by time is called *Baojiang*. In addition to that, the gold articles shouldn't be kept together with the other metal products, and should be dusted by soft brush and wiped by soft antelope skin. Ether, petrol (benzene), neutral soap-suds or ammonia water (10%), can be used for necessary wash, followed by thorough rinse with distilled water and heat dry. Any kind of coating material and rough antelope are forbidden.

- 金带托莫盅
  Gold Cup and Saucer

错金银

错金银又称"金银错",是春秋时期发展起来的一种金属加工工艺,在战国、西汉时期最为流行。其具体做法是先在青铜器表面预先铸出或錾刻出图案、铭文所需的凹槽,然后嵌入金银丝、片,锤打牢固,再用蜡石将其打磨光滑,突出图案和铭文,美化器物。被错金银工艺装饰过的器物的表面,金银与青铜的不同光泽相映相托,将其图案与铭文衬透得格外华美典雅。

Gold and Silver Inlay

Gold and silver inlay started from the Spring and Autumn Period (770 B.C.-476 B.C.), prevailed in the Warring States and Western Han Period. The procedure is to incise patterns or inscriptions on the surface of bronze ware by casting or by chiseling, have gold and silver wire inlaid, and then grind and polish to highlight the patterns and inscriptions. The brilliance of gold and silver matches the shines of bronze very well.

• 错金银龙凤纹带钩
Gold Inlaid Silver Belt Hook with Dragon and Phoenix Pattern

• 错金银铜豹镇
Gold and Silver Paperweight Inlaid Copper Panther

- 错金银神兽
  Gold Inlaid Silver Therion

- 铜错金博山炉
  Gold Inlaid Copper *Boshan* Stove

金银平脱

金银平脱最早产生于汉代,这种工艺做工精细、费工费料,但器物相当精致美观。唐代,贵族们为了炫耀富丽堂皇的生活,在漆器上大量运用金银装饰。其实早在商代就已经出现了用锤打的金片装饰器物的工艺,但由于技术落后,金片只能简单地附着于器物表面。春秋战国时期,这种贴饰技术发展为将金银丝镶嵌入器物表面刻纹中的错金银工艺。汉唐盛世,这一工艺达到了鼎盛,尤其是唐代,工匠们在前人的基础上进行改良,将这种工艺普遍应用于漆器的装饰制作,从

Jinyin Pingtuo

Jinyin Pingtuo craft technique was created in the Han Dynasty (206 B.C.-220 A.D.). Although it cost more material and time, the products are very exquisite and beautiful. In the Tang Dynasty (618-907), the nobles used massive gold and silver to decorate their lacquer wares in order to flaunt the magnificent life. In fact, early in the Shang Dynasty (1600 B.C.-1046 B.C.) there was a technique to hammer the gold leaf onto articles for decoration, but as the lag in technology, gold leaf could just simply be attached to the surface of articles. In the Spring and Autumn and Warring States periods (770 B.C.-221 B.C.), this technique developed into gold and silver inlay technique. By the flourishing Han and Tang dynasties, this technique reached its peak. Especially in the Tang Dynasty, the craftsmen made improvement on the base of the predecessors and widespread the technique in lacquer wares' decoration, finally the technique *Jinyin Pingtuo* was completed. The method is by melting

● 金银平脱镜
Gold and Silver Cutting Mirror

而形成了"金银平脱"技术。其做法是将金银熔化后制成箔片，再裁制成各种纹样，用胶漆粘贴在漆器上，然后髹漆数重，漆干后细加研磨，使金银箔片显露出来，与漆面平齐。

gold and silver to make foils, tailor them into various patterns, paste them on the lacquerware with varnish gums, and then paint lacquer several times. After drying polish to reveal the gold and silver foils to get smooth surface of lacquer wares.

金银平脱与剪纸艺术

金银平脱工艺被广泛应用后，人们利用此技术刻镂金箔，装饰在头鬓上。南朝官员宗懔在《荆楚岁时记》中记载，每年的正月初七是人的节日，在这一天要举行许多特殊的活动来庆祝"人日"。人们不仅要张灯结彩、登高赋诗，还要剪刻金箔及各色丝帛为各种人形，贴在发鬓上以示祝贺。许多家庭还喜欢将剪刻的金银箔片装饰在屏风和窗门上，目的都是为了祈求风调雨顺、万事如意。后来，这些节日里的活动成了窗花艺术的起源。此时的剪刻艺术已经同民间风俗融合在一起，为民间剪纸的产生和发展奠定了坚实的基础。

Jinyin Pingtuo and Paper Cutting

After *Jinyin Pingtuo* was widespread, gold foil cutting was used for hair ornament. An officer of the Southern dynasties called Zong Lin wrote in his book *Records of Annual Functions in Jing-Chu Area* that the seventh day of the first lunar month is Human-day; many celebration activities took place on this day. People put up lanterns and festoons, climbed mountains and wrote poems. Furthermore, they cut gold foils and colorful silk figures and sticked them at temples to celebrate the festival. Many families also liked to decorate their screens, doors and windows with carved gold and silver foils to pray for good weather, harvest, and good luck in everything. These activities were the origin of window paper cutting. At the same time cutting art combined with folk custom and laid a solid foundation for the development of paper cutting.

• 剪纸艺术品
Arts of Paper Cutting

錾刻与模冲

錾刻又称"錾花",始于春秋晚期,盛行于战国以后,是一种在器物成型之后对其表面进行装饰的工艺。其具体方法是用小锤打击各种大小纹理不同的錾刀或錾头,使之在器物表面留下錾痕,形成各种纹样,达到装饰的目的。在金银器使用了锤鍱技术后,錾刻一直作为细部加工最主要的手段而被使用。铸造器物的表面刻划、贴金包金器物的部分纹样也采用此方法。由于錾刻工艺具有独特的装饰效果,所以在现代金属装饰工艺中仍被使用。

模冲也是金银器纹样制作中经常使用的一种工艺,即在金银器物的表面,以事先预制好的模具冲压出凸起的花纹图案。用这种方法制

Engraving and Stamping

Engraving craft started at late Spring and Autumn Period and went popular after the Warring States Period, was a craft to decorate the surface of the articles after being shaped. The method is hammering different gravers to leave carving marks on the surface of articles to form patterns. Since hammering craft has been introduced to the gold and silver articles, the engraving technique is always the major process for detail processing. This method has also been used in the surface carving and partial patterns on gold pasting and gold coating articles. For its unique effect, engraving craft is still used in modern metal decoration.

Stamping is another craft often used in pattern making of gold and silver articles. Use prefabricated moulds to stamp the raised patterns on the surface of the gold and silver

• 模冲银盒
Stamped Silver Box

铜鎏金錾花卉方香炉
Gilding Copper Square Incense Burner with Carved Patterns

錾刻银镀金葫芦式执壶
Gold-plated Silver Gourd-shaped Pot with Carved Patterns

成的纹样富有立体感，明暗对比也非常明显，装饰性较强。

累丝

累丝又称"花丝""掐丝"，是中国传统工艺。其具体做法是先将金银等原料拉成细丝，以焊接、编缀等方法制成纹样，再焊接到器物之上。累丝工艺在我国金银器制作中有着非常久远的历史，早在两汉时期就已达到了相当高的水平，

wares. The pattern formed in this craft has a vivid third dimension, with strong light and shade contrast and decoration effect.

Filigree

Filigree is a form of traditional Chinese craft. The method is drawing gold or silver into fine wire, and welding onto the surface of an object made of the same metal or doing in openwork. The filigree has a long history in China's

- 铜镀金累丝珐琅首饰盒
  Gilding Copper Filigree Enamel Jewelry Box

- 累丝银盒
  Filigree Silver Box

但当时多用以制作小件器物；到了宋代才出现器皿类作品，但仍然极为罕见；明清时期累丝工艺获得了极大的发展，尤其是进入清代以后，其技艺更为精进。其品种不仅有各种首饰，还有瓶、盒以及各式佛龛等。这种工艺多用于制作摆件和首饰，采用制胎、花丝、镶嵌、烧蓝、点翠等多种工艺制成。

gold and silver production industry and reached a high level early in the Han Dynasty (206 B.C.-A.D. 220 A.D.), but was mainly used to produce small articles; by the time of the Song Dynasty (960-1279) some utensils emerged, but were still rarely to be seen; the craft was well-developed in the Ming and Qing dynasties, especially when it came to the Qing Dynasty (1616-1911). The products made in this craft of that time not only include various accessories, but also bottles, boxes, various Buddha shrines and so on. This craft was mainly used to make ornaments and accessories which include processings like base making, wire welding, inlaying, enameling and feather pasting, burning blue, kingfisher, etc.

- 金丝发罩
  Gold Wire Hairnet

银器的保养

银同金一样，也是一种贵重金属，银的提炼技术较金复杂。银是性质相当稳定的金属，在室温或加热情况下几乎看不出与氧或水的作用，但在大气中容易受某些物质的侵蚀，而使颜色变晦暗。

银器也易被空气中的一些物质腐蚀，形成角银（氯化银），呈灰色或带有褐色和紫色。如果仅仅在表面生成一层薄薄氯化银银膜，则呈现出一种悦目的古斑色调，很具古董的味道。这些古斑是稳定的，增加了银器的艺术魅力，尽量不要去处理它，让它保存下来。如果嫌颜色暗，可用软布擦拭，布上蘸一点白垩粉加水调成的糊，或用含有几滴氨水的酒精擦，但最好不要除去银器上一层均匀的"包浆"，这是岁月的痕迹，是因氧化作用而形成的一层附加金属。

　　值得注意的是，置放银器的空间必须保持清洁，没有灰尘和污染；不要用多汗的脏手接触银器，应当小心仔细地把器物上沾染的各种物质清洗掉；除尘和清洁可用软布揩擦，防止银器受到机械损坏。只有在确有把握能改进外观和使纹饰清晰时才能进行处理。

The Maintenance of Silver Articles

The silver is precious metal like gold, but more complex to extract. Silver is pretty stable. It barely reacts with oxygen or water in room temperature or heated. But it is easily corroded by some substance in the atmosphere, and darkens.

　　The silver articles can also be easily corroded by some substance in the atmosphere and generate argentic chloride, which would display grey, brown or purple. If it's only a thin layer of

• 瓜棱形银壶

此银壶束颈，腹呈十二瓜棱状，下为圈足，通体素面，锤镍成形，器表磨光。

Melonridge-shaped Silver Pot

Straight neck, twelve ridges in the belly, ring foot in the bottom, and no pattern on the body, this ware was shaped by hammering and the surface was polished.

• 团花银盒

Silver Box with Round-flower Pattern

argentic chloride film, the hoary spots left on the surface will be looked antique old. These ancient spots are steady, increasing artistic charm, which should be kept as possible as we can. Silver articles can be wiped by soft cloth dipped in whiting paste or alcohol mixed with several drops of ammonia water. But try best not move the *Baojiang*, the additional metal layer caused by oxidation. It's the evidence of age.

Silver wares should be kept in clean rooms without dust or pollution. Never touch silver articles with dirty sweaty hands. Clean carefully to avoid any mechanical damage. Any complex clean for better appearance should not be done unless you are very sure.

• 银锤花嘛呢轮

嘛呢轮是佛教一种祈祷法器，用金、银、铜皮制成，压制有各种花纹图案，内装经卷，并装有可转动的轴，轴枢多以蚌壳做成。

Silver Prayer Wheel with Hammered Pattern

The Buddhist prayer wheel (*Mani* Wheel) is made of gold, silver or copper, pressed with various flower patterns, inbuilt with scripture and rotatable axis. The centre of the axis was mostly made of clamshell.

镶嵌

镶嵌是一种传统的加工工艺，嵌法分为两种：一是包边嵌，有口上平整的一并包边和口上有花纹的花包边；另一种是包脚嵌，有四脚、六脚和多脚等多种。

传统的镶嵌工艺就是把钻石、宝石、珍珠等物嵌到金银饰物上，

Inlay

Inlay is one of the traditional processing crafts and can be divided into two ways: first is rim-covered inlay, including flat rim-covered and patterned rim-covered; second is foot-covered inlay, including 4 feet, 6 feet, multiple feet and so on.

The traditional inlay craft is to enchase diamonds, gemstones, pearls

或者将金银丝镶嵌进红木、牛角、紫檀、铜器、紫砂等器具。镶嵌是一种独特的工艺，制作时先将各种题材的图画粘贴上去，然后沿着图画中的线条造成沟槽，并将与沟槽一样粗细的金丝或银丝嵌进去，最后经过抛光和揩漆，使制品具有精细雅洁的艺术特色。镶嵌工艺历史久远，商周时期就有了镶嵌金器。

on gold or silver articles, or setting gold and silver thread into the articles made of mahogany, ox horn, red sandalwood, bronze, purple clay and so on. Inlay is a specific craft that need to firstly stick paper with pattern onto the base, then cut grooves along the line of the pattern and inset gold or silver thread exactly into the grooves. Polishing and painting would dignify the finished article with elegance.

- 嵌宝金背木梳
Wooden Comb with Gold Ridge Inlaid with Gems

- 金累丝嵌松石高足盘
Gold Stem Plate Inlaid with Turquoise

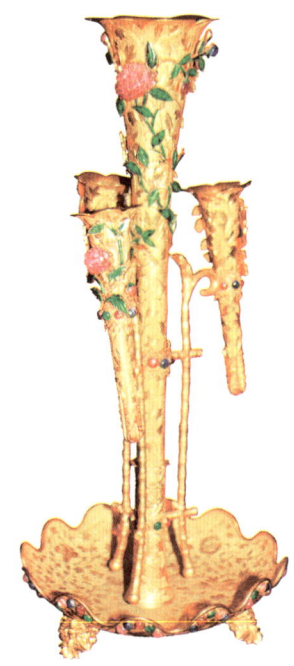

- 金嵌翡翠碧玺花插
Gold Receptacle for Cutting Flowers Inlaid with Jade and *Bixi* (Tourmaline)

炸珠与透雕

炸珠又称"金珠",是中国古代金工传统工艺之一。其制作方法是将黄金、白银熔化,再把金银液倒入水中,利用金银液与水温度的显著差别,使之结成大小不等的小颗粒,然后按照一定的图案将它们焊接在器物表面。炸珠工艺最早出现于三四千年前的地中海沿岸地区,大约在西汉时

This craft has a long history of more than three thousand years. Gold articles with inlaid patterns emerged in the Shang and Zhou dynasties.

Gold Beading and Hollow out Carving

Gold beading is one of the traditional crafts in ancient China. It is an art unique to gold or silver processing which is first to let melted gold or silver drip into

- 花卉纹镂空金钗
  Gold Hollow Hairpin with Flower Pattern

- 掐丝炸珠镶嵌金仕女
  Gold Wire Inlaid Beading Court Lady

传入中国。唐代，炸珠常与掐丝和镶嵌工艺结合，广泛应用于首饰盒装饰类器物上。

透雕，又称"镂空"，就是指用锐利的工具錾刻掉设计中不需要的部分，形成透空的纹样。

点翠与点蓝

点翠工艺是首饰制作中的一个辅助工种，起着点缀美化金银首饰的作用。该工艺的发展在清代乾隆时期达到了顶峰。它的制作工艺极为繁杂，制作时先将金、银片按花形制作成一个底托，再用金丝沿着花形图案的边缘焊个槽，在中间部分涂上适量的胶水，将翠鸟的羽毛巧妙地粘贴在金银制成的金属底托

warm water drop by drop to form beads of various sizes. Then weld each tiny drop of gold or silver articles to form different patterns. This craft was created in the Mediterranean coastal regions about 3 or 4 thousand years ago and was introduced to China among the Western Han Dynasty (206 B.C.-25 A.D.). In the Tang Dynasty (618-907), beading craft was usually combined with filigree and inlay and widely used for decorating articles such as jewellery box.

Hollow out carving is to carve off the needless parts of the design with a sharp tool to form the transparent pattern.

Kingfisher Feather Art and Enameling

Kingfisher feather art is one of the subsidiary crafts in the accessories making which can embellish and beautify the gold and silver accessories. This craft was developed to the peak during the reign of the Qing Emperor Qianlong (1736-1795). The process is extremely

• 银镀金点翠圈锁
Gilding Silver Ring Lock Decorated with Kingfisher Feather

"松鹤延年"纹点蓝金瓶
Enameled Gold Bottle with Pine and Crane Pattern

上，形成吉祥精美的图案。这些图案上一般还会镶嵌珍珠、翡翠等珠宝玉石，越发显得典雅而高贵。点翠的羽毛以翠蓝色和雪青色的翠鸟羽毛为上品。由于翠鸟的羽毛光泽感好，色彩艳丽，再配上金边，以此做成的首饰佩带起来可以更添富丽堂皇的装饰效果。

点蓝工艺又称"烧蓝工艺"，与点翠工艺一样都属景泰蓝工艺。该工艺不是一种独立的工种，而是作为金器的辅助工种以点缀、装饰、增加色彩美而出现在首饰行业中的。使用了点蓝工艺的工艺品晶莹夺目，金碧辉煌，具有浑厚持重、富丽典雅的艺术特色。

complex. First make a flower-shaped bottom bracket with gold or silver leaves, then weld gold wire along the rim of flower and put glue in the central part. After precisely pasting kingfisher feather onto the bracket, an auspicious and beautiful pattern has been made. Pearls or jade are often enchased to make the articles more elegant and noble. The turquoise blue or violet kingfisher feathers are the best for this craft. As kingfisher feathers have magnificent gloss and beautiful color, decorated with golden rim, the accessories made by this craft are very luxurious.

Enameling craft, as same as kingfisher craft is part of cloisonné craft. It is an auxiliary craft for gold article making. It is a cloisonné craft, which creates glittering, luxurious, stately and elegant products.

> 纹饰工艺

金银的自然魅力和永恒价值，使古今中外的人们对它们产生浓厚的兴趣。不过，金银器让人惊艳的不只是它的外形，更在于它那精美绝伦、形式多样的纹饰。这些让人叹为观止的纹饰不但反映了当时的工艺水平、审美观念、文明传承，更折射出当时社会的主流文化。

龙纹

龙是中国古代传说中的一种神兽，龙纹则是中国传统装饰纹样中最具生命力、最富民族特色的题材之一。古人认为龙是最高级的祥瑞，故龙成为崇拜的百神之一。

在中国古纹样装饰中，龙纹占有非常重要的地位，被大量装饰在玉石、牙骨、陶瓷、织绣和服饰等诸多

> Pattern Craft

The natural charm and enduring values of gold and silver attract people at all times and in all over the world. However, the gold and silver articles amaze us not only for their shapes, but also for the exquisite and multitudinous patterns. These beautiful patterns can reflect the craftsmanship, aesthetic standards, civilization inheriting, and the social mainstream culture of that time.

Dragon Pattern

The dragon is a mythical animal in Chinese legends and myths. The dragon pattern is one of the most long-lived and characteristic themes among Chinese classic patterns. The ancients considered dragon the highest auspicious sign and one of the hundred immortals.

The dragon pattern has a very important status in the ancient China's pattern

- **云龙纹金提炉**

  云龙纹描绘的是奔腾在云雾中的龙，即云和龙的共同体，通常将龙的头、尾、脚打散，又和抽象的云融会在一起，显示出一种似云非云，似龙非龙的神秘意境。

  Gold Handled Stove with Dragon and Cloud Pattern

  The dragon and clouds pattern describes the dragon flies in the clouds, as an integrated image. It usually break up the head, tail and feet of the dragon and mix them up with the cloud to display a mystical image.

物件之上。封建社会，龙纹被赋予了新的神秘色彩，尤其在宫廷艺术之中，更是充满了龙的装饰纹样。以龙作为装饰，大体包含了两种含义：一是说龙是水中的灵物；二是说龙为天象的象征，是宇宙的象征。古代农业社会，非常注意天象，而龙则被看作是自然力量的形象化身。

唐代金银器的龙纹多为单独的蟠龙或行龙，四足三爪，阔嘴长须，骧首奋翼，舞爪腾跃。在唐朝，龙还不是皇家专用图案和皇家标志，所以唐代工匠在塑造刻划龙时，主要是从艺术角度去表现，即怎样把龙表现得美，表现得劲健有力、气宇轩昂。到了明朝，统治者对龙纹的使用实行了

decorations, massively used in the decorating of jades, bones, ceramics, weavings, clothes and so on. The decorations of the dragon mainly possess two meanings: firstly the dragon was considered the spiritual animal of water; secondly was considered the symbol of the astronomical phenomena, which symbolized the universe. Dragon here was regarded as the embodiment of the natural power.

The dragon patterns on the gold and silver articles of the Tang Dynasty (618-907) were most single curled-up dragon or flying dragon with 4 feet, 3 claws, wide mouth and long palpus, whose actions were vivid and revved up. The dragon had not been limited within the

垄断，尤其到了清朝对龙纹的使用非常严格，五爪龙纹是严禁民间使用的，三爪和四爪龙纹虽可以使用，但也主要以供器为主。清代金银器的龙纹日趋繁复，作为纹饰的主题，或与其他纹饰配合使用。晚清时的龙纹比起前朝明显变得呆滞，线条纤细简化而无力，龙纹下垂，渐无威严之感。

imperial family in the Tang Dynasty, so the craftsmen of that time did their best to beautify the dragons in art. By the Ming Dynasty (1368-1644), the rulers monopolized the using right of the dragon patterns. When it came to the Qing Dynasty (1616-1911), the restriction on the use of the dragon patterns became more strict, which specified that the five-claw dragon was forbidden in folk, three-and-four-claw dragons could be used only on the confessional articles. The dragon patterns on the Qing's gold and silver articles became more and more complex. Some is the theme of the patterns, may be mixed with other varieties of patterns. By the later period of the Qing Dynasty, the dragon patterns obviously became more lifeless than the previous dynasties, the lines were simpler and less powerful, and the dragons were drooping and lost the feeling of prestige.

Phoenix Pattern

The phoenix was adored as the spirit bird in the ancient totem era which was considered to be an auspicious sign. As a result, the phoenix pattern was widely used to decorate articles.

In the early stage of the Tang

- "二龙戏珠"纹金罐

中国民间有在庆祝佳节时舞龙欢庆的传统，舞时由一人持彩珠与二龙嬉戏，称"二龙戏珠"，通常为两云龙一火球。如果图案为多条龙戏珠，称为"群龙戏珠"。

Gold Pot with *Erlong Xizhu* (Twin Dragons Holding on a Pearl) Pattern

The dragon dance is a traditional activity in China to celebrate the festivals. One dancer holds the colorful ball playing with two dragons, so called "Twin Dragons Holding on a Pearl". Normally there are two cloud dragons with one fire ball. If the pattern contains more than two dragons, it is called "Multiple Dragons Holding on a Pearl".

- **团龙纹金钵**

团龙纹源起于唐代,就是将龙的形体处理为圆形构图,在宋代和明清金银器上普遍运用。其表现形式多种多样,通常饰以水波、如意等,让团龙纹显得华丽而生动。团龙既保持了龙的完整性,又有很强的适用性和装饰性,所以运用十分广泛。

Gold Bowl with *Tuanlong* (Dragon in a Circle) Pattern

The *Tuanlong* (dragon in a circle) pattern was oriented in the Tang Dynasty (618-907), which made the dragons in round structure and was widely used on the gold and silver articles in the Song, Ming and Qing dynasties. The style of this pattern is multiple, usually in water wave or *Ruyi* styles, vivid and magnificent. As the round-dragon pattern can keep the integrity of the dragon with strong feasibility and decoration effect, it was used widely.

凤纹

凤在远古图腾时代被视为神鸟而得到崇拜,它的出现往往被当作一种祥瑞,因此凤纹也被大量用来装饰各种器物。

在唐代的金银器上,早期的凤纹多为单独的立凤,中后期的凤纹多成双配置。其造型主要为朱冠金喙、鼓翼而舞、长尾华美、文采斑斓。在唐代金银器中,龙和凤一般都是单独使用,还没有明显的龙凤配对意识。到了宋元明清时代,龙 Dynasty's gold and silver articles, the phoenix patterns were more in single; in the middle and later period, the patterns appeared more in double. The appearances mostly have a red pileum, gold beak, wide wings, long gorgeous tail and beautiful color. In the Tang Dynasty, dragon and phoenix patterns were used separately on gold and silver articles. By the time of the Song, Yuan, Ming and Qing dynasties, the dragon and phoenix patterns appeared together on the gold and silver articles, symbolizing the emperor and queen of the feudal dynasty.

• 银镀金簪花龙凤耳托杯

龙凤呈祥是中国古代的传统纹饰之一，为一龙一凤。传说龙是鳞虫之长，凤为羽虫之尊。哪里有龙出现，哪里就有凤来仪，哪里就会天下太平，五谷丰登。龙凤都是人们心目中的祥兽瑞鸟，二者常常合在一起，为祥瑞和吉祥的象征。

Gilding Silver Handled Cup with Saucer Patterned with Flowers, Dragon and Phoenix

The "Prosperity Brought by Dragon and Phoenix" has been one of classic patterns since ancient times. This pattern contains one dragon and one phoenix. In Chinese legend, dragon is the king of scaly creatures and the phoenix is the lord of birds. The showing of the dragon and phoenix together will bring the peace and harvest. Both of them are auspicious creatures, the combining of which can be an auspicious sign.

• 凤鸟纹银酒壶

凤鸟纹酒壶的躯体是鸟，头部有一较长的喙。凤鸟纹盛行于商至两周，商代凤鸟纹多短尾，西周多长尾高冠。

Silver Wine Pot with Phoenix Pattern

The phoenix pattern has a bird body and a long beak, which was popular from the Shang Dynasty to the Zhou Dynasty. The phoenix patterns in the Shang Dynasty (1600 B.C.-1046 B.C.) often have short tails, while in the Western Zhou Dynasty (1046 B.C.-771 B.C.) generally have long tails and high pileums.

● 金凤
Gold Phoenix

凤出现在金银器中，象征和比喻封建王朝的帝后。

瑞兽纹

除了龙、凤这两种神兽外，中国古代金银器上还常见其他动物纹饰。这些动物因具有吉祥寓意，称为"瑞兽"。所谓瑞兽纹，即是以某种兽类的图形作装饰以驱避邪恶或预兆凶吉，不同的兽类有不同的含义。常见的瑞兽纹有狮纹、熊纹、鹿纹、龟纹、摩羯纹。

Auspicious Animal Patterns

Beside of dragon and phoenix, other animal patterns also can be seen on ancient China's gold and silver articles, which usually possess an implied meaning of auspiciousness, therefore called the "auspicious animals". The auspicious animal patterns were decorations of some animals which in order to exorcise evil spirits or divine. Every animal has its implied meaning. Regular auspicious animal patterns include the lion pattern, bear pattern, deer pattern, turtle pattern, makara pattern.

● 狮纹银盘

狮子在中国古代称为"狻猊"。在唐代，狮子是最重要的瑞兽，这可能与当时佛教的兴盛有关。狮子在佛教典籍中是护法的祥物。狮子同样也是中亚、西亚金银器常见的装饰题材，唐代金银器上使用的狮纹明显受到外来文化的影响。

Silver Plate with Lion Pattern

Lion was called *Suan Ni* in ancient China. In the Tang Dynasty (618-907), lion was the most momentous auspicious animal, which might relate to the flourishing of the Buddhism at that time. Lion is the auspicious animal to uphold the constitution according to the records of the Buddhism classics. Lion patterns can also be seen often in the gold and silver articles from the Middle and West Asia. The lion patterns on the gold and silver articles in the Tang Dynasty were obviously inspired by the foreign culture.

● 鎏金熊纹六曲银盘

熊在古代以勇猛著称，梦见熊是孕妇生男孩儿的吉兆。在重男轻女的中国封建社会，人们以得子为荣，因此熊纹自然就非常受喜爱。

Gilding Six-petal Shaped Silver Plate with Bear Pattern

In ancient times, bear was famous for its courage. Dreaming of bear was considered to be a propitious sign of the birth of boy. In the China's feudal society, people preferred boys to girls; as a result, the bear pattern was naturally loved by the people.

- 荷叶龟纹银碗

龟一直被古人当作吉祥物来看待，汉代品级高的官印皆为龟纽，唐也以龟纽为官印，武则天时还将鱼符改为龟符。龟有高官厚禄之意，同时龟还是长寿的象征，唐及唐代之前的人喜欢用龟作人名或装饰题材。

Silver Bowl with Lotus-leaf and Turtle Pattern

Turtle was always seen as an auspicious animal in ancient time. The high-ranking official seals in the Han Dynasty (206 B.C.-220 A.D.) all had turtle knobs and such design was been used in the Tang Dynasty (618-907) too. Empress Wu Zetian even changed the fish-shaped tallies into turtle-shaped. Turtle possesses the implied meaning of promotion, rich and longevity, so in ancient times, turtle was very popular for people's name or decoration use.

- 鎏金鹿纹菱花形银盘

鹿在中国古代被认为是纯善之兽，且鹿、禄谐音，有"利禄长存"之意，所以鹿纹一直是古人深为喜爱的纹样。

Gilding Silver Rhombus Flower-shaped Plate with Deer Pattern

Deer have been considered the animal of goodness since ancient China. Besides, as *Lu* (deer) is in Chinese a homophone of *Lu* (salary), which possess an implied meaning of "inexhaustible incomes", the deer pattern was fond by the ancients all the time.

"四鸟绕日"金饰

2001年，四川成都金沙遗址出土了一件"四鸟绕日"金饰，画面为四只神鸟围绕着太阳飞行，被专家命名为"太阳神鸟"。"四鸟绕日"图案是中国古人崇拜太阳艺术表现形式的杰出代表作，用来寓意追求光明、团结向上、奋勇前进、和谐包容，是中国文化遗产的重要标志之一。

Gold Ornament with "Four Birds Surrounding the Sun" Pattern

In 2011, a Gold Ornament with "Four Birds Surrounding the Sun" pattern was excavated from the Jinsha Site in Chengdu City, Sichuan Province. The pattern is four birds flying round the sun, which was named by a specialist the "Sun Bird". This craft is one of the master pieces showing the worship of the sun by Chinese ancients, implying the meaning of the pursuing of light, uniting together, moving forward, harmony and inclusive wisdom, which is selected as one of the major marks of the China Cultural Heritage.

- **"四鸟绕日"金饰** (图片提供：FOTOE)

  "四鸟绕日"金饰外层为四只飞鸟，内层为旋转的太阳，如同一轮旋转的火球，极具动感的视觉效果。"太阳神鸟"图案已经被中国国家文物局用作中国文化遗产标志，并被"神舟六号"载入太空。

  Gold Ornament with "Four Birds Surrounding the Sun" Pattern

  Four birds flying outside of a rotary sun which is like a revolving fireball, is full of dynamic visual effect. The pattern has been selected by the China's National Bureau of Cultural Relic as the mark of the China Cultural Heritage, and went into the space with China's *Shenzhou VI* spacecraft.

植物纹

植物纹是中国古代金银器中表现得最多的题材，既有写实的，也有图案化的。秦汉以前，金银器上的植物纹饰种类较少，隋唐开始明显增多，并且出现了许多外来植物纹样。宋元时的植物类纹饰仍以写实为主，并流行瓜果类装饰。明清

Plant Patterns

The plant patterns are the most popular theme on ancient China's gold and silver articles, some of which are realistic, some are in pattern style. Plant patterns on gold and silver articles from before the Qin and Han dynasties were seldom, but has obviously increased since the Sui and Tang dynasties. At that time plant patterns from abroad appeared. Most plant patterns from the Song and Yuan dynasties are more in realistic style, and fruit-shaped decorations were popular. By the Ming and Qing dynasties, plant patterns were widely used. Patterns of

- 菊花纹银碗

菊花在中国古代被看作花群之中的"隐逸者"，霜寒色更鲜，故常被喻为"君子"。

Silver Bowl with Chrysanthemum Pattern

The chrysanthemum was seen as the "hermit" among the flowers in ancient China. These flowers bloom better when the frost comes, likened to the "man of noble character".

- 卷草纹银酒台

卷草纹是金银器上常用的一种辅助纹样，以柔和优美的波状曲线组成连续的草叶纹样装饰带而得名。

Silver Stand Tray for Wine Vessels with Interlocking Grass Blade Pattern

Interlocking grass blade pattern is a subsidiary pattern often used for decorating gold and silver articles, named by its conterminal grass pattern composed with beautiful soft wavy curve.

时期，植物类装饰趋于图案化，具有文人画特点的松、竹、梅组合较为多见。金银器上的植物纹主要包括忍冬纹、缠枝纹、团花纹、折枝花纹、宝相花纹、莲叶纹、绶带纹等。

combination of pine, bamboo and plum blossom which possesses the feature of paintings were very popular. The main plant patterns on gold and silver articles include Reineckea Carnea pattern, interlocking branch pattern, posy pattern, floral sprays pattern, composite flower pattern, lotus-leaf pattern, ribbon pattern and so on.

- **掐丝团花纹金杯**

团花是一种泛称，一般指外轮廓为圆形的装饰纹样。在金银器中，这类花朵均是一朵盛开花瓣的正视形或俯视形，由中心多层次地向外展开，交错叠压。团花纹在隋唐时期最为流行，形象更显丰美，成为一种特色的装饰纹样，后人称之为"唐草"。

Filigree Gold Cup with Posy Pattern

Posy pattern is the general name of the patterns with round-shaped outline. This kind of pattern always is the front or bird-eye view of a blooming flower which unfolds from the center layer upon layer. The posy pattern was most popular in the Sui and Tang dynasties, whose shape was beautiful and plump and developed to a specific decoration pattern. The later generations called it "Flower of Tang".

- **金錾牡丹鞢**

牡丹花种类繁多，以色彩绚丽、芳姿艳质、天然姣美被冠以"花中之王"，享有"国色天香"的盛誉。牡丹纹是古代金银器经典装饰纹样，多在瓶、罐、盘、缸等大器造型上运用，被视为繁荣昌盛、美好幸福的象征。

Peony-shaped Gold Fingerstall with Carved Patterns

Rich in variety and colors, peony is called the King of Flowers, with which people praise it as "national beauty and heavenly fragrance". The peony pattern is one of the classics in ancient gold and silver article decoration pattern and often used to decorate large-sized articles like bottles, pots, plates, jars and so on, which was considered as the symbol of prosperity and happiness.

• 莲瓣纹银托盏

莲瓣纹是中国古代传统的纹饰之一，早在西周时期已应用于青铜器上，多装饰于器物颈、肩、足等部位。莲花又称"佛花"，寓意高贵纯洁，是在佛教文化影响下流行的纹饰。

Lotus-shaped Silver Calix with Saucer

Lotus petal pattern is one of the ancient China's classic patterns, was firstly found on the bronzes from the Western Zhou Dynasty (1046 B.C.–771 B.C.) and is mostly used to decorate the neck, shoulder or foot of articles, implying the meaning of dignity and purity, which went popular by the influence of the Buddhist culture.

• 铜镀金皮球花三人打乐钟

皮球花又称为"小团花"，是一种不规则的呈放射状或旋转式圆形纹样。皮球花盛行于明清两代，青花、粉彩、斗彩、珐琅彩都常常使用这类纹样。

Gilding Copper Desk Clock with Three Musicians and Ball-shaped Flower Pattern

Ball-shaped flower pattern is also called "small posy", which is an irregular radial or rotary round pattern. This pattern was flourishing in the Ming and Qing dynasties, and often used on blue-and-white porcelain, powdered-color porcelain, contending-color porcelain and enamel-color porcelain.

• 葵花纹金盏

葵花纹也是中国古代传统的纹饰之一，最早出现在瓷器中，后来才被引用到金银器上来。

Sunflower-shaped Gold Calix

Sunflower is also a traditional pattern in ancient China, firstly used to decorate porcelain before it was used on gold and silver articles.

人物故事纹

人物故事纹是指以人物活动或人物形象为内容的纹饰。人物故事纹又分为两类，一类是反映历史人物的图纹，如描写姜太公钓鱼的故事。另一类是反映现实社会生活的图纹，以狩猎纹最为多见；再如童子嬉戏图纹表现了儿童的天真活泼，有斗草、乐舞等；仕女生活题材尤为多姿多彩，有乐伎、戏婴、梳妆、游乐等；也有乐舞人物，他们穿戴不同，手持各种乐器；还有反映古人信佛崇佛的飞天、菩萨、罗汉、释迦牟尼等佛教形象。虽然人物故事纹在金银器中并不少见，但数量远没有动物纹和植物纹多。

Character and Story Patterns

The character and story pattern is composed with human activities or characters, which can be divided into two varieties: the first type is patterns reflecting the historical personages, like the story of the Fisher King; the other type is patterns reflecting the realistic social life. For example, the hunting pattern was mostly used; the children playing patterns displayed their naive and lively features; the life of the maid patterns were especially varied, which included the activities like music playing, playing with kids, dressing, making up and so on; musicians wearing clothes in various styles and playing all kinds of instruments also can be seen often; further more there were patterns of the religious images like Bodhisattva, arhats, Sakyamunic and so on. Although character and story patterns are not rare on gold and silver articles, its quantity is far more less than animal and plant patterns.

• 金錾花阁楼人物八角盘
Gold Octagon Plate with Carved Pavilion and Figures Pattern

弦纹：杯腹上部饰一道凸弦纹，下部阴刻一道弦纹，高足中部有凸起圆环，上刻联珠纹一周。

String Pattern: A raised carving string pattern decorated on the upper belly and a diaglyph string pattern on the lower part. A bulgy ring set in the middle of the high foot, on which carved a circle of conterminal bead pattern.

狩猎纹：口沿下刻有一周缠枝花，两道弦纹之间饰有骑马狩猎图四幅。猎者均策马飞驰，姿态各异，或张弓待射，或箭方离弦；被追逐的獐、鹿、豕、狐等动物则神情惊慌，四散逃窜，整个狩猎场景布局巧妙，情节紧张生动。

Hunting Pattern: A circle of branch and flower patterns carved below the rim, four riding hunting pictures decorated between the two bowstrings. The hunters are whipping the horse and riding swiftly in different gestures; the roebuck, deer, pig and fox as the chased animals are in panic and scattering in all directions. The overall arrangement of the whole hunting image is delicate and the story is lively and intense.

缠枝花纹：杯体近底处亦饰有一周缠枝花，圈足外表饰宝相花。

Interlocking Branch Pattern: A circle of branch flowers is decorated near the bottom of the body, and the surface of the ring foot is covered with composite flowers pattern.

- 狩猎纹高足银杯

狩猎纹在金银器中较为常见，一般为猎人纵马驰骋，弯弓持械，追逐猎物。此银杯锤击成形，錾刻纹样，直壁深腹，下有托盘，接外撇高足。该银器纹饰满密，繁而不乱，以四幅狩猎图最为精彩。

Silver Goblet with Hunting Pattern

Hunting pattern can be seen in gold and silver articles, which usually is the image of a hunter riding a horse with a blow and chasing a prey. This one was hammered on its shape and carved with pattern, and has a straight side, deep belly, a pallet in the bottom attached to the bulgy high foot. This pattern is complex but not mussy; the most wonderful parts are the four hunting pictures.

几何纹

几何纹是一种最原始的纹饰，由几何形的线形组成，具有线形变化和结构变化构成的形式美感。常用于金银器的几何纹有连珠纹、弦

Geometric Pattern

Geometric pattern is one of the most initial patterns, formed by the lines of geometry, with the beauty of the transforming in linear and structures. The most popular geometric patterns

- **金錾花云雷纹圆盘**

  云雷纹是金银器上传统的纹饰之一。云纹用柔和回旋的线条组成，雷纹用方折角回旋的线条组成。

  Gold Round Plate with Carved Cloud and Thunder Pattern

  Cloud and thunder pattern is one of the most classic patterns used on gold and silver articles. The cloud pattern adopts soft whirly lines and the thunder pattern is composed with dog-leg whirly lines.

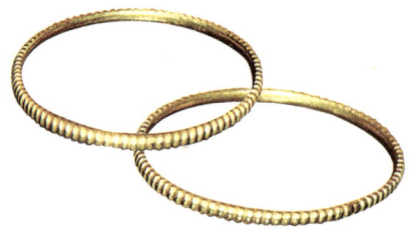

- **连珠纹金手镯**

  连珠纹是用小圆圈作横式排列而产生的纹样，又叫"带圈纹"，最早出现在青铜器上。连珠纹一般用作主纹的分栏线，或作为兽面纹的边饰。

  Gold Bracelet with Conterminal Bead Pattern

  Conterminal bead pattern is formed by the tiny beads arranged in horizontal type, which was first found on bronze. This pattern is usually used as the halving line of the major pattern, or the rim decoration of an animal face pattern.

- **弦纹银壶**

  弦纹是金银器上最简单的纹饰之一，为一根凸起的直或横的线条，在大多数情况下用作界栏。有的金银器上仅有弦纹，没有其他纹饰，简洁朴素。

  Silver Pot with String Pattern

  String pattern is one of the simplest patterns on the gold and silver articles, which is a bulgy straight or transverse line, mostly used to be the halving lines. Some gold and silver articles are only decorated with string pattern, which are very compact.

纹、直条纹、横条纹、斜条纹、云雷纹、乳钉雷纹、曲折雷纹、勾连雷纹、三角雷纹、菱形雷纹、网纹菱形雷纹、网纹、贝纹等。

used in the gold and silver articles are conterminal bead pattern, string pattern, needle line pattern, horizontal stripe pattern, slanted stripe pattern, cloud and thunder pattern, studs thunder pattern, flexural thunder pattern, T-type thunder pattern, triangular thunder pattern, rhombic thunder pattern, web rhombic thunder pattern, web pattern, shell pattern and so on.

兽面纹

兽面纹是一种带有宗教色彩的纹样，常见于先秦时期的青铜器，形象为正面表现的兽头，旧称"饕餮纹"。饕餮是中国古代神话中的一种怪兽，长有一张大嘴，十分贪吃，见到什么就吃什么，因此饕餮纹常用于食器上。

Beast-face Pattern

Beast-face pattern is an auspicious pattern with religion concerns, often appeared on bronzes from pre-Qin Period (before 221 B.C.). The pattern was formed by a front view of the animal head and called *Taotie* Pattern in the past. *Taotie* is a beast in ancient Chinese mythologies, which has a large mouth and is very fond of eating. So *Taotie* pattern is usually used on cooking and dining utensils.

- 饕餮纹圆尊
  Enamel Round *Zun* (Wine Vessel) with *Taotie* Pattern

吉祥图案

吉祥图案是指具有一定吉祥寓意的装饰纹样，起源于商周。明清时期，吉祥图案几乎发展到了"图必有意，意必吉祥"的地步。金银器常见的吉祥图案有如意纹、八宝纹、杂宝纹、开光纹、双喜纹、寿字纹、福寿纹、珠联璧合、万字纹、万寿无疆等。

Auspicious Patterns

Auspicious patterns represent patterns with certain auspicious signs, oriented from the Shang and Zhou dynasties. By the Ming and Qing dynasties, the auspicious pattern has developed to a level that every pattern has implied meanings which must be auspicious. The common auspicious patterns appeared on gold and silver articles including *Ruyi* pattern, eight treasures pattern, miscellaneous treasures pattern, *Kaiguang* pattern, double happiness pattern, character of longevity pattern, happiness and longevity pattern, perfect pair pattern, boundless longevity pattern, and so on.

- **如意纹银瓶**
  如意纹是如意形的装饰纹样，借喻称心如意。
  Silver Vase with *Ruyi* Pattern
  The *Ruyi* pattern impliedly means that everything will go as one wishes.

- 双喜纹金碗

  双喜纹是文字纹的一种，即将"囍"字加以图案化，施用于瓷器、布帛、家具、木雕等器物之上，作为装饰，寄寓了双喜临门，喜上加喜之意。

  Gold Bowl with Double Happiness Pattern

  Double happiness pattern is one of the character patterns. Design the character of happiness in different patterns and put on porcelain, cloth, furniture, woodcarving, meaning more happiness.

- 金錾团寿纹手镯

  团寿纹即由多个"壽"字纹组成，多施用于瓷器与布帛之上，金银器上也并不少见。

  Gold Bracelet with Carved Round-Longevity Pattern

  The round-longevity pattern is composed with multiple characters of longevity and is common on porcelain, cloth, gold and silver articles.

- 八宝双凤纹金盆

  八宝又称"八吉祥"，寓意八宝的纹样常见的有珠、球、磬、祥云、方胜、犀角、杯、书、画、红叶、艾叶、蕉叶、鼎、灵芝、元宝、锭等，可随意选择八种，不同历史时期所常用的八宝纹也有所不同。

  Gold Basin with Eight Treasures and Double Phoenix Pattern

  The eight treasures was also called the "eight auspiciousness", which usually choose eight objects from pearl, ball, chime stone, auspicious cloud, *Fangsheng* (a type of geometric pattern), rhinoceros horn, cup, book, painting, red leaf, folium artemisiae argyi, banana leaf, *Ding* (cauldron), glossy ganoderma, gold ingot and so on. The combinations of the eight treasures are different in different historical periods.

• 银錾福寿纹执壶

福寿纹是中国古代的传统纹饰之一。图案通常由蝙蝠、寿桃或团寿组成，是以蝙蝠谐音福，以寿桃或团寿喻示寿，福寿纹于清雍正、乾隆朝较为盛行。

Silver Ewer with Carved *Fushou* (Happiness and Longevity) Pattern

It is one of the classic patterns, usually composed with bats, peaches and round-longevity. The character bat and happiness have the same pronunciation and tone in Chinese. Peaches in the design are a symbol of longevity. This pattern was flourishing in the period of Emperor Yongzheng and Emperor Qianlong of the Qing Dynasty.

金银器的器形
The Shape of the Gold and Silver Articles

　　中国古代金银器的器形有很多，不同器形的外在形象和轮廓都是当时特定的历史文化的反映。传统金银器主要包括饮器、食器、容器、茶具、装饰品等几大类。

The various shapes of the ancient China's gold and silver articles reflect the specific historical and cultural environments. The traditional gold and silver articles can be divided into several major categories, which are the drinking vessel, dining utensil, container, tea set, ornament articles, ect.

> 饮器

饮器是指饮酒、饮茶和饮水用的器皿。其种类有杯、壶、羽觞、茶托、盏等，以杯的数量和种类最多。

常见的金银杯可分为高足杯、长杯、带把杯等。高足杯的器口为圆形或多曲圆形，杯体之下接高足，高足中部一般有一个被学者称为"算盘珠"式的节，下部向外撇

> Drinking Vessels

The drinking vessels are utensils used for wine, tea and water, which include cup, pot, *Yushang* (birdy cup), saucer, and calix. Among these, cup has the most variety and quantity.

Common gold and silver cups can be divided into goblet, long cup, and handled cup. The rim of goblet is a round or twisted circle, with a high foot

• **鎏金银鸡冠壶**

此壶为辽代金银器中之精品，壶把为鸡冠形状，壶盖与壶身以银链相连，盖面錾刻对称的四瓣花纹，外沿錾刻八个四瓣花朵；壶颈较高，四周錾有牡丹纹。壶身鼓起，两面錾刻精巧，均在菱形图案中錾有一只花鹿，鹿前后各饰山石、灵芝、海水，犹如仙境；壶身前面成三角形，三条边作仿皮绳纹装饰。

Gilding Silver Cockscomb-shaped Pot

This pot is one of the masterpieces among the gold and silver articles of the Liao Dynasty. The handle is cockscomb shape and the cover is connected to the body with a silver chain. The surface of the cover is carved with symmetric four-leaved flower pattern with eight four-leaved flowers carved on the outer rim. The neck is high and the circle of the neck is carved with peony pattern. The body is bulgy, both sides are carved with a spotted deer within the rhombic pattern. Stones, glossy ganoderma and seawater are carved surrounding the deer, which is as beautiful as heaven. The front view of the body is in triangle, the three sides of the triangle are imitating leather lines.

• 金樽

此金樽呈八棱形，秀美挺拔，棱线流畅。金樽的两侧刻有攀缘相向的立体龙纹，用蓝琉璃镶眼珠，起到画龙点睛的效果。一龙首向下，用白银镶双翼；一龙首向上，用白银镶双角，金银相映，奇趣无比。樽身錾刻精细的装饰纹样，用连续刻出的点组成线条，花纹细如毫发。

Gold *Zun*

This gold *Zun* is octagon with smooth line and beautiful tall shape. On the sides carved with two solid dragons scrambling opposite direction. The dragons' pupils are made of blue glass, bringing the artwork to life. One dragon facing down with silver inlaid wings; the other facing up with silver inlaid horns, while the gold and silver set each other off beautifully. The body was carved with detailed pattern of the conterminal lines and spots, as fine as hairs.

呈喇叭状。杯用来盛装液体，器足具有放置和使用时手执的功用。长杯的杯口大多呈椭圆形和多曲椭圆形，体形较长，杯腹较浅，内壁有凸起的条棱，外壁则向内凹陷，杯

attached to the bottom of the body. In the middle of the high foot usually decorated with a joint called the "Abacus Bead" by scholars, and the lower part of the high foot spread out form a trumpet shape. The body is used to contain liquid and the foot of the ware is used to stand and hold by hand. The rims of the long cups usually are oval or twisted oval and the body shapes long with a shallow cup and a ridge bulged on the inner side and the outer surface indents. The bottom of the body is usually attached with a ring foot, which is also called "ring-foot cup". The most obvious feature of the handled cups is the handles different in shape on one side of the cup bodies. Generally this kind of cup has deep body with ridges, and a ring foot in the bottom. However it doesn't belong to the shape of Chinese traditional article. In line with the archaeological discoveries, some of which were imported from Sogdiana (now within the territory of Uzbekistan) located in the Middle Asia, and some were copied by the ancient Chinese craftsmen in accordance with the articles introduced from the Sogdiana.

The varieties of the gold and silver pots are rich too, which have multiple purposes. Some of them were used to

体下一般附圈足，故又称为"圈足杯"。带把杯最显著的特征是杯身一侧有不同形制的把手，杯体较深且大部分有折棱，底部有圈足。然而中国传统器物造型中没有带把杯，从出土的金银器带把杯来看，有些直接是从中亚粟特（位于今乌兹别克斯坦境内）等地输入的，也有一些是中国古代工匠模仿粟特等地器物而制造的。

金银壶的种类也较多，用途各不相同，有些用作饮器，有些为容器。常见的金银壶器形有提梁壶、带盖壶、三足或四足壶等。

羽觞即耳杯，最早出现于东周，盛行于汉代。羽觞呈雀鸟状，浅腹、平底，两侧有半月形双耳，

drink, and some used as containers. The conventional gold and silver pots are handled pot, covered pot, three-leg or four-leg pot and so on.

Yushang (birdy cup) also called *Er Bei*, appeared in the Eastern Zhou Dynasty (770 B.C.-256 B.C.) and flourished in the Han Dynasty (206 B.C.-220 A.D.). Birdy cup is named by its shape like a bird, with shallow belly, flat bottom, and double half-moon-shaped ears on the both sides, sometimes the cup can also be pie-shaped or has high feet. The body shapes of *Yushang* are different

• 瑞兽纹盏托

此盏托为圆形，唇边以范铸与錾花手法制成，盘沿为二方连续回纹一周，盘心为一双钩篆书"壽"字。盘心与盘沿间为半浮雕式海水江崖瑞兽纹，水中有若隐若现的马、龙、狮、象、鱼等瑞兽。该盘在制作上突出整体的效果，不拘泥于细部的刻画，呈现出浑厚、粗犷的风格。

Cup Saucer with Auspicious Animal Pattern

The saucer is in round shape, whose lip is made with molding and carving crafts, rim is decorated with a circle of conterminal double-squares, and the center of the plate is carved with character "Longevity" in double hooked seal character. The space between the center and the rim is decorated with semi-relief of seawater, cliff and auspicious animals. Horse, dragon, lion, elephant and fish can be seen indistinctly in the water. It intends to highlight the integral effect but not the details, which displays a sincere and rough style.

有时也有饼形足或高足，因其左右形如两翼而得名。羽觞形状因时代不同而各有所异，比如两汉时期的羽觞呈椭圆形，两侧呈半月形耳，以后逐渐变椭圆形为两沿略尖微上翘如船形。

in various periods. For example, the ones from the Han Dynasty (206 B.C.-220 A.D.) are oblate-shaped with half-moon-shaped ears on both sides, which generally transform into the boat-shaped with rims raising slightly.

曲水流觞

"曲水流觞"是中国古代流传的一种饮酒游戏。古人每到农历三月初三就会在弯曲的水流旁设酒杯，即羽觞。羽觞顺流而下，流到谁的面前，谁就拿起来饮，并作诗一首。东晋永和九年（353年）三月初三，王羲之携亲朋好友数十人，相聚会稽山阴（今浙江绍兴）的兰亭，举行曲水流觞的游戏，饮酒咏诗，所作诗句编成了《兰亭集》，王羲之还为其作序。从此，曲水流觞，咏诗论文，饮酒赏景便流传下来，历经千年而不衰。

Floating Wine Cup along the Winding Water

"Floating Wine Cup along the Winding Water" is an ancient drinking game. In ancient times, on the 3rd day of the third lunar month, people would get together and place a *Yushang* (wine cup) in the winding water. The cup floats down the water, and then stops in front of a player, who should drink the wine in the cup and make a poem. On the 3rd day of the third lunar month of the 9th years of Yonghe in the Eastern Jin Dynasty, Wang Xizhi, a master of calligraphy, gathered dozens of friends at Lanting Pavilion in the north side of Kuaiji Mountain (now Shaoxing City, Zhejiang Province) and played the aforementioned game, drinking and inditing. The collection of poems wrote on that day is *Lanting Ji* (*Orchid Pavilion Poems*), and Wang Xizhi wrote the preface for the collection. Hence, the game together with chanting poems, drinking and enjoying views of spring scenery has lasted for thousands of years.

- **玉耳金钏**
  此羽觞呈椭圆形，敛口，卷沿，腹微鼓，平底。两耳为玉质，呈圆环形（断面方正），饰卷云纹，铆接于近器口两侧。

  Gold *Yushang* with Jade Ears
  It is oval, contracted mouth, curved rim, slightly bulgy belly and flat bottom. The ring-shaped ears are made of jade, decorated with curved cloud pattern, riveted on sides near mouth.

盖：盖饰云纹，圈足饰行龙赶珠及海水江崖流云纹；盖顶嵌玉，并镶一石榴子红宝石为纽，纽以金链与把相系。

Lid: The lid is decorated with cloud pattern, with the ring foot covered with flying dragon chasing bead, sea-water, cliff and floating cloud patterns; a garnet ruby is inlaid as a knob, which connected to the handle with a gold chain.

颈：颈部刻如意云纹，方形腹部、把、流两面刻二龙戏珠纹，另两面在玉龙上下四角饰海水江崖及流云纹。

Neck: The neck is carved with *Ruyi* cloud pattern, Two Dragons Hold on a Pear pattern on the handle and mouth sides of the belly, and sea-water, cliff and floating cloud pattern on the other two sides surrounding the jade dragons.

肩：肩部镶嵌红、蓝宝石数块，腹部的把、流两侧，各镶嵌玉雕盘龙一条，龙睛及龙额部分各嵌红宝石三块。

Shoulder: The shoulder is Inlaid with several rubies and sapphires on the shoulder, and two jades coiling dragon on each side of belly, three rubies on dragon eyes and forehead.

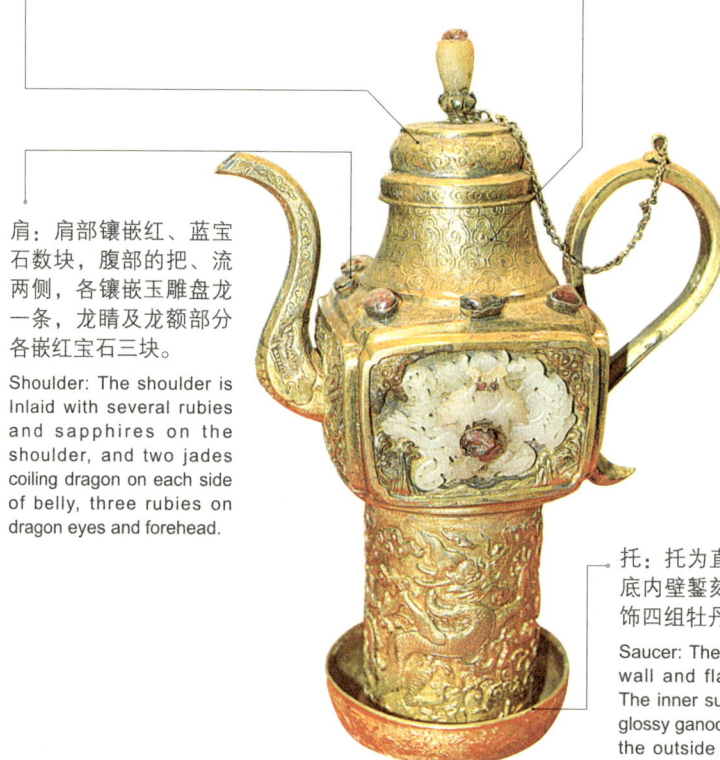

托：托为直壁平底浅盘形，底内壁錾刻灵芝花，外侧壁饰四组牡丹花卉纹。

Saucer: The saucer has straight wall and flat shallow bottom. The inner surface is carved with glossy ganoderma flower pattern; the outside is carved with four sets of peony patterns.

- 带托金酒注

此酒注为直口，粗颈，方腹，圆筒形高圈足；一侧附耳形把，另一侧有细长流。整个酒注造型新颖别致，气度端庄华丽，具有浓厚的宫廷色彩，制作工艺复杂精致，为明代金器之杰作。

Gold Wine Pot with Saucer

With straight opening, thick neck, square belly, cylinder-shaped high ring foot; ear-shaped handle and thin long-mouth, this pot is novel and delicate, which displays an elegant and luxuriant royal style. With a complex and delicate craft, this pot is a master piece of the gold articles in the Ming Dynasty.

金玉良缘

自古以来，金和玉就有着不解之缘，常常合制成一件器具。"金玉良缘"是一个成语，用来借指姻缘前世注定，十分美好。关于"金玉"的成语还有很多，如金玉满堂、金玉良言、金枝玉叶等。

Jinyu Liangyuan (Good Relationship like Gold and Jade)

The gold and jade have been bounded together since the ancient times, which were always combined together in articles. People always describe a happy and fated couple as beautiful as gold with jade. There are a lot of phrases with gold and jade in Chinese. *Jinyu Mantang* (gold and jade fill the house) means abundant wealth. This phrase is also used in the praise of a talented person. *Jinyu Liangyan* (gold and jade words) means golden sayings, *Jinzhi Yuye* (gold branches and jade leaves) means honorable status.

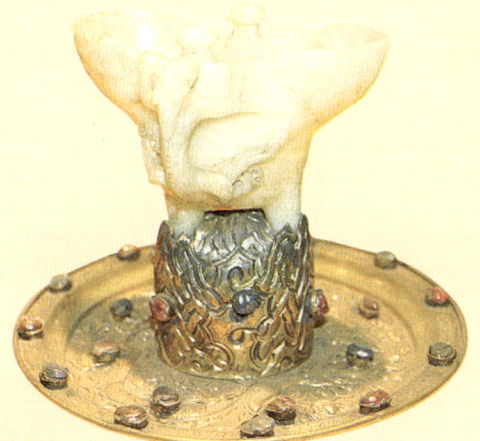

- 金座玉爵

此金座实为金盘，纯金，采用锤击成型，平錾花纹。主要纹饰为作腾跃状的金龙，周围镶嵌红宝石，盘沿四周饰有云头纹。爵身以白玉雕成，下承镶宝石金座。爵和托盘（金座）均镶红蓝宝石。白玉、红蓝宝石与黄金交相辉映，真可谓珠光宝气，富丽堂皇。

Jade *Jue* (Wine Cup) with Gold Base

The gold base is actually a pure gold saucer, shaped by hammering, carved with patterns. The major pattern is a gold dragon ready to fly. Ruby inset surround the dragon and cloud pattern decorates the rim. The body of the cup is carved from a piece of white jade, attached to the gold base inset with gems. The cup and the plate (gold base) are all inset with rubies and sapphires. The white jade, gems and gold add radiance and beauty to each other, creating a luxurious image.

口：杯口錾刻回纹，一面正中开光，阳文篆书"金瓯永固"四字，另一面折"乾隆年制"款识。

Mouth: Its edge is carved with square spiral pattern and with the characters *Jin'ou Yonggu* (unimpaired territorial integrity) in seal script amid them on one side and the characters *Qianlong Nianzhi* (made in the Qianlong reign) on the other.

耳：两侧立夔龙为耳，龙头顶端嵌珍珠一颗。

Handle: Handle is built in the shape of *Kui* dragon with a pearl on its head.

足：三个卷鼻象头为足，以金丝象牙环抱。

Legs: Three legs are shaped in rolled trunk elephant heads hemmed in gold wire ivory.

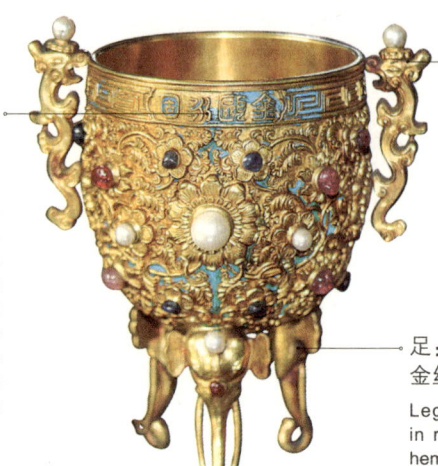

- 金嵌珠宝"金瓯永固"杯（清）

此杯是清代皇帝在元旦举行的开笔仪式上专用的酒杯，造型雅致、纹饰精美。此杯呈斗形，花纹对称，并以珍珠、红蓝宝石作花蕊，精细规整，光洁晶莹，古雅别致。

Gold *Jin'ou Yonggu* Cup Inlaid with Pearls and Precious Stones (Qing Dynasty, 1616-1911)

This gold cup was for the exclusive use of the emperors in the Qing Dynasty on New Year Ceremony. Its body features patterns of composite flowers, and inlaid with pearls, rubies and sapphires at the center of flowers which are fine standardized, glittering and unique.

- 金錾花嵌珠杯盘

这套金质杯盘为清宫内务府造办处所制，华贵富丽，是宫廷举行大宴时供皇帝使用的。带有"萬壽無疆"赞词的清代金质酒杯目前还很少见。金杯呈圆形，口大，深腹，腹下部收敛，平底。杯外壁錾行龙，龙身侧为缠枝莲纹，近足处有海水纹。杯两侧各有一耳，耳上部为莲花托，托上嵌大珍珠一颗，其下部镂空篆字；一耳为"萬壽"，一耳为"無疆"，字下有灵芝纹。托盘较阔，宽沿，其上錾缠枝莲，嵌有珍珠数颗。

Gold Wine Cup and Saucer with Carved Patterns and Inlaid with Pearls

It was made by the Construction Bureau under the Imperial Household Department for the exclusive use of the emperor at grand banquets at the court. Not many gold wine cups with eulogy of *Wanshou Wujiang* (May Your Majesty Enjoy Boundless Longevity) are found up to now. This cup has round shape, wide mouth, deep constringent belly and flat bottom. The outside is decorated with a carved walking dragon against a background with patterns of intertwining lotuses. The portion near the bottom features patterns of waves. The cup has two handles, each topped with a carved lotus flower with a large pearl embedded in it. One handle bears the hollow carved characters in seal script *Wanshou*, and the other *Wujiang* above glossy ganoderma patterns. The saucer has large wide flat and wide edge, on which are carved intertwining lotuses graced with several pearls.

- **金錾云龙纹执壶**

此执壶是清代皇帝举行大典或宫廷宴会时的御用酒具，以金锤制而成，壶身较高，细颈，圆腹，喇叭形圈足。腹壁一侧有细长而弯曲的流，另一侧有环状曲柄。口部加尖塔形壶盖，宝珠纽，盖纽与曲柄之间有金链相连。壶体呈瓜棱纹，每一棱纹内錾刻上下两组立龙戏珠的图案，共30条，龙体曲折盘绕，活泼、灵动。

Gold Ewer with Carved Cloud and Dragon Pattern

This ewer is a wine set used by the emperors of the Qing Dynasty on the major ceremonies or royal parties. The ewer is hammered with gold, with tall body, thin neck, round belly and trumpet-shaped ring foot. On one side of the belly there is a thin long and curving mouth, on the other side there is a cyclic curly handle. The opening is spire-shaped covered with a gem knob, which connects to the curly handle with a gold chain. The body has melon-ridge pattern, within every two ridges carved with two sets of vertical dragon playing bead patterns up and down. There are 30 dragons in all, whose curly bodies are very lively and clever.

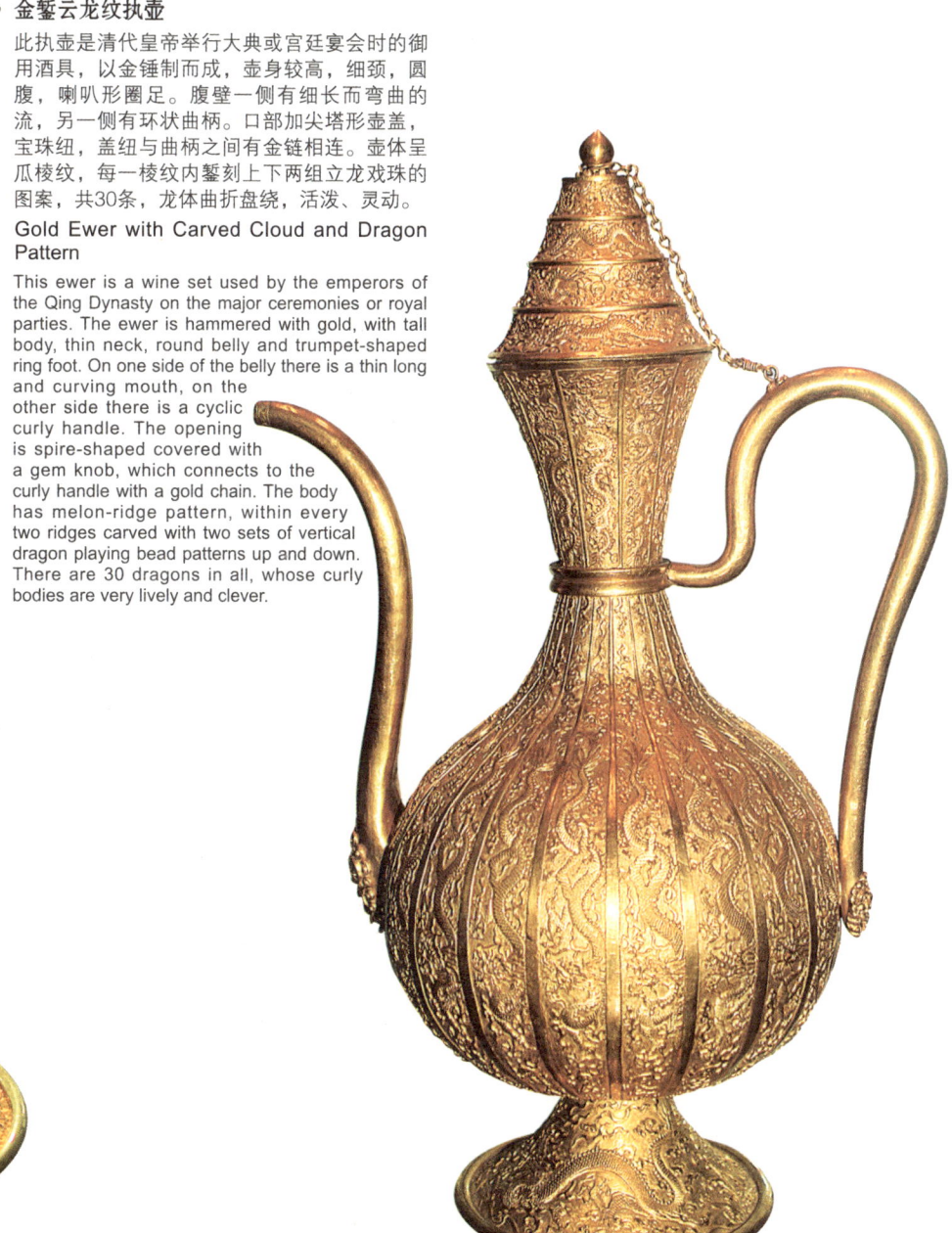

纹饰：通体錾刻纹饰，从上至下分三组，每组四面的中心均为一朵大宝相花，周围六朵小宝相花，枝叶相连，花朵均鎏金。葫芦体上半部有两道弦纹，弦纹之间为两周枝叶纹。

Pattern: Patterns are carved all over the body. They are divided into three groups from up to down. Every group has a big gilded composite flower surrounded by six small ones at the center of four sides with consecutive branches and leaves. Two string patterns separated by branch-leaved patterns circle the upper part of the gourd.

盖；塔形盖，盖上錾刻莲瓣纹，盖上有纽。

Lid: Lid is tower-shaped, carved with lotus-leaf pattern, on which has a knob.

流：腹部凸出一龙首吐长流，相对一侧有龙首吐曲柄。

Mouth: A dragon head bulges out of the belly and erupts a long mouth. On the opposite another dragon head erupts the curly handle.

- 银錾花葫芦式执壶

此壶为银质鎏金，葫芦式，形体巨大，造型规整实用，是皇帝出游打猎时的用品，为乾隆时期大型银器中的佼佼者。

Silver Gourd-shaped Ewer with Carved Patterns

This gilded silver ewer is shaped like a gourd, the size is huge and the shape is standardized and practical, which was used by the emperor for hunting and was one of the master pieces of large silver articles during the Reign of Qianlong.

多穆壶

多穆壶原是西藏、青海地区藏族人民盛酥油茶或酒的一种银制品。酥油茶是在茶砖熬成的浓茶中倒入少量的酥油和盐，有的还加入牛奶，是藏族同胞生活的必需品。

Duomu Pot

The *Duomu* Pot was a kind of silver ware used by the Tibetans in Xizang and Qinghai areas to fill the buttered tea or wine. The buttered tea is made of the strong tea boiled from the camellia bricks and poured with a spot of butter and salt. Sometimes other condiments like milk are added, then stir till the water and butter mixed. This is one of the daily necessities of the Tibetan compatriots.

- **银镀金龙凤纹多穆壶**

  此多穆壶，口部有花冠形装饰，软链式柄，壶流较短，圈足，壶体上有龙凤纹装饰。这类造型颇为奇特的多穆壶过去一般是宫廷或蒙、藏上层人士家庭盛放奶茶用的。

  Gilding Silver *Duomu* Pot with Dragon and Phoenix Pattern

  This *Duomu* pot has corolla-shaped decoration on the mouth, soft chain type handle, relatively short pot mouth, short foot, and dragon and phoenix pattern on the body. This style of *Duomu* Pots with peculiar shapes was usually used by the royal court or the upper circles of Mongolian and Tibetan in the past.

> 食器

　　古代食器种类很多，用金银制作的食器主要有盘、碟、碗、盏、筷子等。

　　盘和碟是金银食器中数量最多的器形，因它们形制接近，可统称为盘；一般形体较大的称盘，较小的称碟。此类金银食器有圆形、菱形、海棠形、葵花形等，盘底一般有平底、圈足、三足等。

　　碗也是金银器中十分常见的器具，主要有多曲碗、带盖碗、折腹

• 银筷子
Silver Chopsticks

> **Dining Utensils**

The variety of the ancient dining utensils is rich, but the major gold and silver articles are plate, saucer, bowl, cup, chopsticks and so on.

　　The plates and saucers are the most popular ones among the gold and silver dining utensils, and as they are similar in shape, they can be jointly called the plate; usually the ones with bigger size are called *Pan* (plate), the smaller ones are called *Die* (saucer). They are in shapes of round, rhombic, malus spectabilis flower, sunflower and so on. The bottom can be flat, ring-foot, three-leg and so on.

　　Bowls are common, including multi-curved bowl, covered bowl, folded belly

碗：碗为白玉质，洁白如脂。圆形撇口，外壁素无纹，内壁琢藏文；碗底有"乾隆年制"四字款。

Bowl: The bowl is made of snow white jade. It has a round shape, wide mouth with an inscription in Tibetan inside and four characters means "Made in the Reign of Qianlong" on the bottom.

盘：盘内壁开光，内饰缠枝纹并嵌松石花；盘中部泛起圆形碗座，其壁錾勾莲纹并嵌松石梅花。

Plate: The inner face of the plate has a clear open against background pattern, in which flower-shaped turquoise are inlaid with interlocking branch pattern. In the center is a round stand for the bowl, also carved with hooked lotus pattern and inlaid with plun-shaped turquoise.

托：托较高，下足圈筒式，下粗上细，其外饰凸起的勾莲纹和数排如意纹，并嵌有松石海棠花、如意纹；上足为圆形托盘，边沿饰连球纹并嵌松石边线。

Support: The high support is in cylinder style, of which the low part is thicker and the upper part thinner, decorated with bulgy hooked lotus pattern and several circles of *Ruyi* pattern, inlaid with turquoise; The upper foot is a round plate with the edge decorated with conterminal ball pattern and inlaid with turquoise.

盖：碗盖略高，宽沿，中部隆起，饰勾莲纹并嵌松石饰片。上有莲花纽，盖顶中部饰重瓣仰莲一朵，花的四周以云头纹相衬。

Cover: The cover is a little high, with wide edge. Its center bulges, decorated with hooked lotus flowers and inlaid with turquoise motifs and its crown is shaped like a lotus flower, which is surrounded by cloud pattern.

- **金錾花高足白玉盖碗**

此器由金托、玉碗、金碗盖三部分组成。托与盖用纯金制成，锤打成半圆形。清代宫廷使用的盖碗种类繁多，金、玉组合的作品则较少。此盖碗金工精致，玉质绝佳，托、盖、碗混为一体，既实用又有很好的陈设效果。

White Jade Bowl with a Gold Cover and Support Decorated with Carved Patterns

It consists of three parts, the jade bowl and gold cover and support. The support and the cover are made of pure gold and hammered into half-round shape. Though the covered bowls were widely used in the palace during the Qing Dynasty, very few of them were made of gold and jade. The gold craft of this bowl is delicate and the quality of the jade is among the best. The bowl and its cover and support are made with superb workmanship and combined perfectly. They are not only aesthetic but also of practical use.

碗、弧腹碗；碗底多有圈足，也有圈底碗。从出土的情况来看，银碗居多，金碗数量较少。

bowl and bow belly bowl, mostly with ring foot. Most excavated bowls are made of silver, while gold bowls are not in big amount.

- 莲瓣纹刻花金碗
Gold Bowl with Carved Lotus-petal Pattern

- 牡丹如意云纹金盏
Gold Calix with Peony and *Ruyi* Pattern

- 银镀金累丝玉瓦嵌珠宝如意
Filigree Gilt Silver *Ruyi* Inlaid with Jade and Gem

> 容器

中国古代容器的种类很多，金银器中主要有盒、罐、盂、盆、药具等，其中盒的出土数量最多。

古代的盒形状多变，有圆形、菱形、云头形、莲瓣形、葵形、海棠形、蝶形、菱弧形、龟背形等，有些盒还带有圈足，尤以圆盒、花瓣盒最多。容器形制分别为上下两部分，可以开启闭合。盒的用途较

> Containers

There are a variety of ancient containers. Gold and silver ones are box, jar, *Yu* (food container), basin, medicine utensils. Boxes are mostly found in the excavations.

The boxes made in ancient times are in many shapes, such as round, rhombus, cloud, lotus-petal, sunflower, malus spectabilis blossom, butterfly, diamond-curve and turtle. Some have ring foot. Most of them are round and petal-shaped. The boxes have lids that can be opened and closed. Boxes were used in many purposes in ancient times. The Large ones were used to keep medical herbs, tea, spidery and other valuable objects; and small ones were usually mainly used

• 仰莲座银罐
Silver Jar with Lotus-shaped Base

广，一般形体较大的盒用于盛放各种药物、茶、香料和其他珍贵的物品；形体较小的主要用于盛放化妆品。用于盛放药物的盒子，其上大多有墨书题记，以标明所放药物的名称和重量等。

罐有素面提梁罐、莲瓣纹提梁罐，除此之外，还有三足罐。罐多用来盛放酒、水，也有用来盛放药材的。

药具主要为炼丹或煮药的器具，如药壶、药铫、药勺等。

to keep makeup. The medicinal herb container often has scripts to mark the name and weight of the medicine in the box.

The jars can be divided into plain jar with loop handle, lotus-petal pattern jar with loop handle and three-foot jar. They were mostly used for wine and water, some were used to keep save the medicines too.

The medicine utensil refers to tools for making pills of immortality or brewing medicinal herbs, such as jar, pot and spoon.

● 金镶宝石圆盒

此圆盒用金成色较高，盒上以镂雕、镶嵌两种工艺组成不同的纹饰，镶有翠、蓝宝、红宝、碧玺等上好的各色宝石。盖边嵌碧玉菊花，盒底有"宝华""足金"戳记。

Gold Round Box Inlaid with Precious Stones

This box is made of gold in high purity, and decorated with hollow carving and inlaid with jades, sapphires, rubies and *Bixi* (tourmaline). The edge of the cover is inlaid with jade chrysanthemums. The marks of "*Baohua*" and "*Pure Gold*" are on the bottom.

● 金漱盂

此器乃宫廷卫生用具，形似今天的痰盂。这件金漱盂是清代皇帝漱口的专用漱盂，通身遍刻双"囍"和"壽"字，应为皇帝大婚时所用。

Gold Washing *Yu*

Very much like today's spittoon, this gold *Yu* was used by the emperor for mouth rinse. The character *Xi* (happiness) and *Shou* (longevity) were carved all over. It was probably made for the wedding of the emperor.

颈：瓶颈为全瓶最细之处，为瓶口的开放及全瓶精神的升华作了铺垫，艺师最后以较细于圈足的粗银丝凝重而遒劲地顺着开放中的瓶口之花勾上了完工的一笔，圆满无缺，可谓是精美绝伦。

Neck: The neck is the narrowest part of the vase, connecting the opening to the body and upgrading the spirit of the ensemble. The craftsman finished the work by the powerful drawing with a thick silver wire on the rim of the opening flower, which perfectly completes the excellent job.

腹：瓶形同样由最膨胀夸张的瓶腹一路上升并缩小至瓶颈，十二道明显的凹槽也随着由宽变窄，向上收缩，使银丝瓶如丝织物般产生出优美的褶皱；同时，这十二道凹槽呈较粗黑的直线，体现了一种力度美，与银丝花纹的极度轻盈形成强烈对比，集金属的坚硬感和蕾丝花边般的轻柔于一身。

Belly: The body dwindles from the bulgy belly to the neck, and the twelve obvious grooves also narrows down from bottom to top, which forms beautiful wrinkles like the silk fabrics. Meantime the twelve grooves are in wide and dark straight lines, which represent the beauty of force and contrast with the lissome silver silk pattern. The combination embodies the strong and tough feeling of metal and the soft of the lace.

圈足：圈足下缘的银圈规整粗壮，增强了银瓶的稳定性；圈足以较小的花纹组成，并随着圈足的向上收缩，花形也愈加纤细，从而强烈地衬托出下坠、丰硕的瓶腹。瓶腹的花纹最大，但镂刻得有如蝉翼般空灵、剔透，且圆转婉妙。

Ring foot: The silver circle on the edge of the ring foot is thick and regular which increases the stability of the vase; the ring foot is composed with smaller patterns of flowers, with the shrinking of the foot the flowers shape more slim, which strongly contrast the drooped and plump belly. The patterns on the belly are carved as fine as the cicada's wings.

- **银累丝花瓶**

此花瓶为敞口，束颈，颈部以下渐广，蒜头形鼓腹，下有外撇式圈足。花瓶作菊瓣形，共分十二瓣，均分瓣累丝而成，然后焊接而成。器形轮廓线是由反转S形曲线构成，线条婉转流畅，具有运动美感。

Filigree Silver Vase

Garlic bulb shaped with twelve petals, it features a neck much narrower than the body with wide mouth and expanded ring foot. Each petal is wire-twined separately and put together by welding. The outline is composed by reversal S-shaped curves, smooth and dynamic.

> 茶具

中国古代的饮茶之风极盛，饮茶方式也极为考究，茶具因此日趋齐备和精美。唐代饮茶之风极为盛行，唐人不仅乐于茶道，而且讲究饮茶用具。古代茶叶的形制与烹饮方法与如今大不相同。当时的茶叶为茶饼（团茶），饮用前需先炙烤茶饼，使之干燥（称为"炙茶"），然后再经碾、罗，使之成

> Tea Sets

Tea was flourishing in ancient China, people paid much attention to the tea drinking method and tea sets were more and more completed and sumptuous accordingly. Especially in the Tang Dynasty (618-907), drinking tea was so popular that the ancients are not only obsessed in Teaism but also particular abont tea sets. The shaping and brewing method of tea were different in ancient times from the present one. The caky tea

- **鎏金银茶匙**
这件茶匙形似勺，椭圆形，微凹，长柄，上宽下窄，稍曲。柄背錾有"二两"二字，为御用。

Gilding Silver Tea Spoon
This tea spoon is oblate, slightly concaved, long handgrip, whose top is wide and the bottom is slim. The back of the handgrip is carved with characters "*Erliang*", which indicates that the spoon belonged to the royal family.

为茶粉。当茶碾成粉后，还要放入罗子里筛，分开精粗，以便贮用。古代的金银茶具种类很多，包括茶罗子、茶碾子、盐台、笼子等，制作十分精致，每件都是精美的工艺品。

(lump tea) need to be baked dry (called "roasting tea"), then ground and sieved into fine or rough power. There were many kind of ancient gold and silver tea wares, including tea sieve, tea roller, salt plate, cage and so on. They are all the work of arts made with delicate crafts.

- 梅花瓣形银茶托

此茶托的托盘口沿稍高于盏口，素面无饰，做工也极规整。

Plum blossom Petal-shaped Silver Saucer

The plate edge is a little higher than the cup edge. It is plain without any pattern but the craftsmanship is very neat.

- 鎏金银荷叶托盏

此托盏的造型与以往的托盘没有什么差别，但最特别的是托盘呈荷叶的形状，周沿微微高起并稍有卷边，一条条隆起的叶筋分外显眼。托与盏的里里外外，均素洁无饰，只在盏口和高而外撇的圈足底部落地处，都加有鎏金条饰一道，宽窄虽依其所在不同各有妙处，但在保持茶具洁净的作用上则是相同的。

Gilding Silver Cup with Lotus-leaf-shaped Saucer

The distinguished feature is the lotus-leaf-shaped saucer. The plate edge is slightly curved with bulgy venations. From inside to outside, the saucer and the cup are totally plain, on which the only pattern are 2 gilding strips decorated on the rim of the opening and the bottom of the ring foot, which are designed for sanitation needs.

从法门寺出土的金银茶具看唐代茶文化

中国的茶文化发展到唐代，饮茶的方法、程序等都更加讲究，也更加精致。唐代煮茶注重技艺，饮茶注重情趣，在许多喜茶文人的诗文中都记载了会聚宾客、品茶论理时的幽雅情景。同时，唐代宫廷的茶艺，规格更高，场面也更加盛大，使用了大量的金银茶具，精美之极。

1987年，陕西扶风法门寺地宫出土了唐代系列宫廷茶具，其中大量金银茶具让人惊叹不已。这套茶具包括茶碾、茶罗、笼子、盐台等。从茶碾、茶罗等錾有铭文的茶具来看，这些茶具制作于唐咸通九年至十二年（868-871），由"文思院造"。文思院是唐代宫廷专门制造金银犀玉器具的手工工场，铭文说明这些茶具是专门为宫廷制作的。这些茶具质地贵重，做工精良，造型华美，是唐代茶文化兴盛的综合体现，堪称茶具中的国宝。

Gold and Silver Tea Sets Excavated from the Famen Temple and the Tea Culture of the Tang Dynasty

When the tea culture of China developed in the Tang Dynasty, the method and procedure of the tea drinking became more delicate. The skill of the tea brewing and the environment of the drinking were took seriously. Many literati's poems have expressed the elegant scenes of people gathering together, tasting tea and discussing with each other. In the meantime, the tea artistries in the palace of the Tang Dynasty had higher standard and grander scenes, where massive of gold and silver tea sets were used.

- **鎏金银调达子**

调达子是用来调茶和饮茶的器具。这件调达子以钣金成型，纹饰涂金。盖沿面饰有蔓草，盖面边缘錾水波和莲瓣纹，中心为宝珠形纽，下衬一周莲瓣纹。此件器具最精美的地方便是腹壁中部刻有吹乐、舞蹈的伎乐纹饰。此外，圈足也饰有花纹，呈喇叭形。

Gilding Silver *Tiaodazi*

It is a utensil of tea mixing and drinking. This one is modeled with metal plate with painted gold patterns. The rim of the cover is decorated with creeping weed, the edge carved with water wave and lotus-petal patterns and there is gem-shaped knob in the center. The most delicate part is the belly with carved musicians and dancers. And the trumpet-shaped ring foot is decorated with flower patterns.

In 1987, many series of tea wares that were used in the imperial court in Tang Dynasty were excavated at Famen Temple in Fufeng, Shaanxi Province, the large quantity of gold and silver tea sets amazed the specialists. This series of tea sets include tea grinder, tea screener, tea cage, salt plate and so on. According to the scripts on the tea roller and tea sieve, these wares were made in the 9th to 12th years of Xiantong Period of the Tang Dynasty and by the "Institute of *Wensi*". This institute was a workshop specialized in making gold, silver and jade articles for the imperial court. These tea wares are made of precious materials, with excellent craft and in beautiful shapes, which can comprehensively reflect the flourishing of the tea culture in the Tang Dynasty and be the master pieces among the tea sets.

碾轮：碾轮中心插置执柄，碾轮中心较厚，边缘渐薄，周边凿出横向齿槽，以便碾轧。

Rolling Wheel: The middle part is thicker and a handle stick is inserted through the middle. The thinner edge is carved with transverse groove for grinding.

碾槽：碾槽卧置于碾座之中，弧形尖底，横剖面呈"V"字。

Rolling Groove: The groove is set within the base, with bow shape and sharp bottom, the cross section is in V-type.

碾座：碾座为长方形，横剖面呈"Ⅱ"状，其顶面台板和底板均较碾槽宽大，以此增强碾座的稳定性。

Rolling Stand: The stand is in rectangle shape, the cross section in Ⅱ-type, and the upper and bottom platens are both wider than the crushing groove, which increases the stability of the crushing base.

- 鎏金银茶碾、碾轮

这是陕西扶风法门寺地宫出土的唐代系列茶具之一，为碾茶时所用。这件茶碾一改当时民间茶碾的正方体造型为长方体，更适应碾茶之需，而茶碾加盖，也更符合卫生要求。

Gilding Silver Tea Roller

This is one tea ware of the series excavated from Famen Temple Site, was used for grinding tea cakes. It is in the shape of cuboid instead of cube, which was used by ordinary people. The improvement and the newly added cover make the processing more convenient and sanitary.

盖：盖体稍隆，盖与盖沿的交棱线为金丝盘旋成的连珠，盖中心为金银丝编成的浮屠状装饰物。

Cover: The shape of the cover is bulgy; the intersection ridge of the surface and rim is conterminal balls weaved out of gold wire; the center of the cover is the Buddha shaped decoration weaved from gold and silver threads.

提梁：提梁用素银丝结为复层，系结于器身两端。

Loop Handle: It is weaved with plain silver wire in multiple layers and attached to the both sides of the body.

器足：器足由鎏金银丝盘旋成三个旋圈套，似爪形笼脚，足上部为兽面装饰。

Feet: The feet are three spin traps weaved with gilt silver wire, shape like claws; the upper parts of the feet are decorated into animal faces.

- **鎏金银笼子**

此笼是盛装茶叶的器皿。笼子由上盖、提梁、笼体和足四部分组成，皆用金银丝编织而成。丝径极细，纹样呈长六角形透空，孔眼如蜂房状。此笼出土于唐地宫，是懿宗所赐整套茶具中的一件，因此弥足珍贵。

Gilding Silver Tea Cage

This cage is a container of tea, composed with cover, loop handle, body and feet, all weaved with very thin gold and silver thread. The pattern is long hollowed hexagons with honeycomb style oylets. It was excavated from the underground palace of the Tang Dynasty and is one of the series of tea sets granted by the Emperor Yizong of the Tang Dynasty, making it very precious.

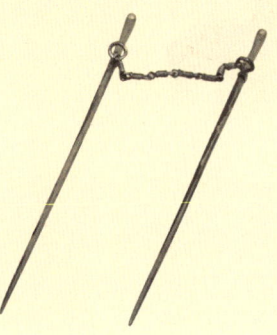

- **银火箸**

火箸是用炉子生火煮茶时，供取炭的器具。这件银火箸通体呈圆柱形，上粗下细，链用银丝编成。

Silver Fire Chopsticks

It is used for picking coal to light stove to brew tea. These fire chopsticks are in cylinder shape, with thick top, slim bottom, and chain weaved by silver wires.

顶盖：顶盖面錾两体首尾相对的飞天，身侧衬以流云。盖刹四侧及立沿饰卧云，罗架两侧饰头束髻、着褒衣的执幡驾鹤仙人，前后两侧錾相对飞翔的仙鹤及云岳纹，四周饰莲瓣纹。

Cover: The surface of the cover is carved with two flying Apsaras connected each other in the heads and tails, beside which decorated with floating cloud. The rim and four broadsides are covered with horizontal cloud. The front and back sides of the frame are decorated with immortals riding with cranes and the other two sides of the frame have flying cranes, cloud and mountains patterns, with the edges of the four sides decorated with lotus-petal pattern.

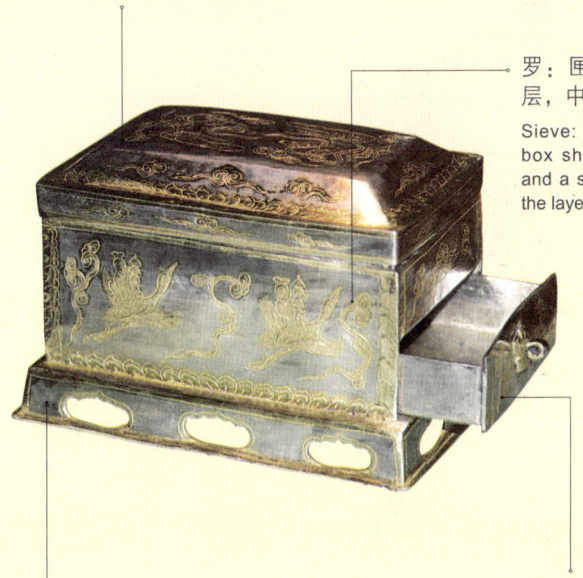

罗：匣形，分内外两层，中央罗网。

Sieve: The sieve has a box shape, two layers, and a sieve net between the layers.

器座：罗架下焊台形器座，四周为镂空的桃形壶门。

Stand: The stand is welded to the bottom of the frame; the four sides are hollowed out in the shape of peach.

屉：屉面饰流云纹，有梅花形衬垫的拉手，用来承接过罗的茶末。

Drawer: The outer surface of the drawer is decorated with floating cloud pattern and has a handle with plum-shaped pad. The drawer is used to put sieved tea powder.

- 鎏金银茶罗

此茶罗为长方体，由盖、罗、屉、罗架、器座组成，纹饰鎏金。

Gilding Silver Tea Sieve

This tea sieve is in the shape of cuboid, composed with the cover, sieve, drawer, frame and base, decorated with gilding patterns.

盖：盖上有中空的莲蕾提手一个，有铰链，可开合为上、下两半，并与盖相焊。中空的提手，通常是放胡椒粉用的。与之相连的盖心，饰有团花一周，还饰以摩羯四尾，盖沿为卷荷形。

Cover: The cover has a hollow lotus-bud-shaped knob which is hinged to the cover. The hollowed knob is usually for pepper. The center of the cover that connects the knob has a circle of round-flower pattern. The cover is also decorated with four makara pattern and curly lotus shaped rim.

台盘：盖下是一个与之相配的台盘，用于存放食盐。

Plate: Under the cover there is a suitable plate used to keep salt.

三足架：三足架与台盘焊接，整体形似平展的莲蓬莲叶；支架以银管盘曲而成，中部斜出四枝，枝头为两花蕾、两摩羯。

Three-leg stand: The stand is welded to the plate, shaped like a flattened lotus leaf. The legs are formed by curly silver pipes. In the center grows 4 branches, with 2 buds and 2 makara attached to the top of the branches.

- **鎏金银盐台**

盐台是古人煎茶调味时存放盐、胡椒等佐料的用器。此三足盐台由盖、台盘和三足架组成。

Gilding Silver Salt Plate

The ancients used it to keep condiments such as salt and pepper for tea making. This one is composed with the cover, plate and three-leg stand.

> 装饰品

　　古代金银装饰品的种类非常多，包括发饰、耳饰、颈饰、手饰等。以发饰的种类数量最多，主要有钗、簪、梳、步摇、金钿等；耳饰主要为耳坠；颈饰主要为项链；手饰主要有手镯、戒指、臂钏等。

> Ornaments

Gold and silver ornaments were in many kinds even in ancient times, such as hair ornament, ear ornament, neck ornament, and hand ornament. Among them the headwear is the most in variety and quantity, mainly including *Zan* (hairpin), *Chai* (two-forked hairpin), comb, *Buyao* (shaking-while-walking hairpin), *Jindian* (a type of hearwear), etc. Ear ornament mainly refers to earrings and neck ornament usually includes necklace. The hand ornament can be roughly divided into bracelet, ring and arm ring.

- 丝束葫芦形金耳坠

此金耳坠为葫芦形，以锤鍱、錾花、焊接等工艺制成。葫芦空心，棱角突出，上端有五个圆珠组成的花瓣，通过缠绕的金丝连接五片蕉叶，葫芦底作钱纹。

Gold Wire Bound Earrings in Gourd Shape

This pair of eardrops is in gourd shape, made by hammering, carving and welding crafts, which is hollow and covered with projecting edge. The top is decorated with 5 petals composed with beads and attached five banana-leave through the twining gold wire separately, the bottom of the cucurbits are decorated with money patterns.

• 金扣腰带

此金扣腰带呈长方形，系铸造成型，并加錾刻。主纹为二猛兽噬一马，马呈伏卧状，两猛兽死死咬住马的颈部和背部，将其捕杀于地；周围有八只圆睛、尖耳、勾喙的禽鸟。

Gold Motif on Belt

This rectangular motif is casted into rectangle with carved patterns. The major pattern is two beasts biting a horse. The horse lies prone, while the beasts bites the horse on its neck and back to the ground, surrounded by eight birds with round eyes, sharp ears and hooked beaks.

• 金镶九龙戏珠手镯

此镯以金栏划分成九格，每格中各錾一团龙，龙口衔珍珠各一。手镯边沿錾刻海水纹，做工精致，具有很强的浮雕效果。

Gold Bracelet Inlaid with Nine Dragons Sporting with Pearls

This bracelet is divided into 9 segments by the gold hurdles. A dragon in a circle with a pearl in the mouth is carved in each portion. The edge of the bracelet is carved with seawater patterns, which is crafted precisely with fine embossment.

• 金镶珠石松竹灵寿簪

此簪为金质，其上有点翠，錾刻加累丝五个灵芝形花朵，上嵌碧玺等红宝石，篆书"寿"字中间嵌东珠一粒，并有松枝及竹叶点缀其中，簪另端为镂空累丝长针状。

Gold *Zan* Inlaid with Pearl Turquoise Pine, Bamboo and Character "Longevity"

This *Zan* is made of gold, five glossy ganoderma decorated made with Kingfisher craft, carving and filigreeing, on which inlaid with rubies. In the middle of the seal, character "Longevity" is inlaid with an eastern pearl and pine-branches together with the bamboo leave are decorated among it. The other end of the *Zan* is hollowed with filigree long pin.

金冠

中国古代的男子都会留发，成年后需把头发绾起，梳成发髻，所以要用冠固定。戴冠时用簪横贯于发髻之中，冠有缨下垂而系于颈间；小冠则不用缨只用簪，以横贯髻中固定。并不是所有成年人都能戴冠，只有士大夫以上的达官显贵才能戴，而且什么人戴何种冠基本上也都有规定。因此，冠不仅有固发功能，同时也是古代典礼时所戴之礼帽，即身份地位的象征或礼仪装束的标志。金冠只有皇帝才可佩戴。

Gold Crown

In ancient China male adults wore long hair and coiled up their hair into a bun. So the crowns were needed to fix the hairdos. To wear a crown, first, stick hairpin through the crown together with hair bun covered in it, and then tie the tassel under chin. A hairpin is enough to fix small crowns. The crowns were not for all men, but only for high officials and noble lords in accordance with prescribed rules about styles and material. Thus the crown was not only used to fix hair, but also the symbol of one's social status and the etiquette attire. Gold crowns are exclusively worn by the emperors.

- **明代万历皇帝金丝冠**

此金冠用极细的金丝编成翼兽的形式，檐内外镶有金口，冠的后上方高耸的部位，精心设计两条金龙，盘绕在透明的金丝网面上。金龙左右对称汇合于冠顶部，龙首在上方，张口吐舌；龙身弯曲盘绕，呈现动势；双龙首中间有一圆形火珠，构成了双龙戏珠的图案。整个金冠双龙飞舞，凶猛威严，象征着封建帝王至高无上的权威，是中国现存的唯一的帝王金冠。

Gold Crown of Emperor Wanli of the Ming Dynasty

This gold crown is made of very fine gold thread woven into a flying auspicious animals and decorated at the back towery part with two dragons. The bilateral symmetrical flying dragons coil at the transparent gold thread net and meet at the top sporting with a fire ball, fierce and dignified, symbolizing the supremacy of emperor's power. This is the only left emperor gold crown found in China.

金簪

　　簪是古代男子固定冠或妇女插髻的首饰，清代妇女尤其喜欢发簪。从清代后妃遗留的簪饰看，不外乎实用型和装饰型两种。实用型簪多为光素长针挺，质地多为金、银、铜等，在盘髻时起到固定头型的作用；装饰型簪多选用质地珍贵的材料制作成图案精美的簪头，专门用于发髻固定后戴在明显的位置上。清宫后妃头簪多用金、玉珠、宝石制作，工艺考究，造型精美。

Gold *Zan* (Hairpin)

The *Zan* was the hair ornament for women and men to fix the topknot, especially loved by women in the Qing Dynasty (1616-1911). According to the ones left by the queens and maids of the Qing Dynasty, they are in two kinds practical style and decorating style. The practical-styled *Zan* is mostly plain and has a long needle made of gold, silver or copper and so on. The decorating-styled one is often made of precious materials with complicated and beautiful patterns, especially for putting on the distinct part of topknot. The queens, princesses and imperial concubines preferred to adorn their hair with *Zan* made of gold, jade and precious stones, which have delicate style and craftsmanship.

● 金嵌珠连环花簪

此簪身錾刻连环状，顶端一环弯曲，上嵌一粒珍珠，另一端呈长尖形。

Gold *Zan* Inlaid with Pearl and Interlinked Floral Patterns

The body was carved into connective rings. The top ring curves and is inset with a pearl, while the other end is in long tapering shape.

金扳指

扳指是古代男子射箭时套在拇指上帮助拉弦的工具。这种具有实际使用功能的饰品，后来逐渐演变成上至王公将相、下至平头百姓皆喜爱的饰品。扳指的材质多为白玉、翡翠、黄金、白银、水晶、碧玺等。

Gold Thumb-ring

The thumb-ring was a tool that men put on their thumb to help pull the string when shooting arrows in ancient times. It later evolved into an ornament loved by people from all levels. Most thumb-rings were made of high-class materials like white jade, emerald, gold, silver, crystal and *Bixi* (tourmaline).

- **金双喜字扳指**

此扳指里外层皆纯金质，中间夹以木质内胆。外层环绕金圈镂雕五个双喜字，均匀排列，上、下边沿各饰一周回纹；内层金圈刻有"义和""足金"两戳记。"义和"即清代中晚期出售金银首饰的私营商号；"足金"即金器中含金量最高的成色。

Gold Thumb-ring with "Double Happiness" Pattern

This thumb-ring is made of pure gold inside and out, and the interlayer is filled with wood as the liner. The outer surface is evenly carved with five characters means "Double Happiness" in a circle, with two circles of fret patterns decorated on both edges of the surface; the inner side is carved with two marks. One is "*Yihe*", the other is "Pure Gold". "*Yihe*" refers to the name of a private trade house dealing gold and silver accessories in the middle and later period of the Qing Dynasty. "Pure Gold" represents the highest gold purity in gold articles.

> 其他器形

金银器的种类繁杂，除了上述器形，还有一些杂项，主要是指一些出土较少又不常见或难以归类的器物，如渣斗、熏炉、熏球（又名香囊）、筹筒、酒令旗、箱笥的铰链、合叶、把手和装饰品等。

> Other Articles

The variety of the gold and silver articles is very complex. Except for the aforementioned shape, there is some articles cannot be classified, which mainly are some rare excavations or articles hard to be classified. For example, the refuse vessel, burner, smoked ball (also called sachet), counter tube, wager game flag, box gemel, hinge, handle, other decorations and so on.

- 郢爰

"郢"是春秋战国时期楚国的国都，"爰"则是重量单位或楚国金币的专有名称，郢爰铸造于约2500年前。此币呈板形，币面铸有供分割成小块的印痕，使用时凿下小块支付，每小块重约15克左右。其含金量一般在九成以上，有的甚至高达99%。

Yingyuan

Ying was the capital of the Chu Kingdom in the Spring and Autumn and Warring States periods, and *Yuan* was the proper name of the gold coin used in the Chu Kindom. The *Yingyuan* was casted 2500 years ago. This coin is in board shape, whose surface is casted with mark lines for the segmentation. Usually a small piece weighting around 15 grams was cut for payment. The gold purify rate of *Yinyuan* was usually more than 90 percentage. Some of them can even be 99 percentage.

- **"和硕智亲王"金印**

  和硕智亲王为清仁宗皇帝次子，嘉庆十八年册封为智亲王；嘉庆二十五年继承皇位，即道光皇帝。此金印近正方形，以龙首、龟身的赑屃为纽。印面阴刻篆为阳文，一半为汉文，一半为满文，共十二字。

  Gold Seal of "Prince Zhi"

  Prince Zhi was the second son of the Emperor Renzong of the Qing Dynasty. Inherited the throne in 1820, he was called the Emperor Daoguang. This seal is in square shape and the shape of the knob is *Bixi* which has dragon head and turtle body (with the dragon claws and tails). The seal face is incised with 12 characters of inscriptions, half in Chinese, half in Manchu alphabet.

- **武则天金简**

  此金简呈长方形，正面镌刻双钩楷书汉字63个，内容为武则天乞三官九府除罪，并有"太岁庚子七月甲寅"纪年。此金简为一代女皇武则天在嵩山所投的祈福除罪金简，是在其自称"圣神皇帝"改国号为"周"10年后，久视元年77岁时所为，是一件十分珍贵的文物。

  Emperor Wu Zetian's Gold Slip

  This gold slip shapes rectangle, with 63 double hook regular script characters carved on the front side. The content is pray for god's blessing and absolution. It was contributed by Emperor Wu Zetian at Mount Song when she was 77 years' old, which was 10 years after she called herself the "Holy Emperor" and turned the title of the reigning dynasty into "Zhou". This is a precious cultural relic.

• 金鹤香薰

金鹤香薰是清廷大殿堂中的重要陈设品。此鹤为金质，呈昂首站立状，通身錾刻羽纹，腹部空，其上履羽翅为盖；鹤的空腹内可以贮香料，香气通过张开着的鹤口飘出；底置一山石形铜铅座，鹤双足底出榫，可插于底座之上。

Gold Incense Burners in Crane Shape

Gold incense burners in crane shape were important furnishings in the big hall of the Qing court. This pair cranes are made of gold, standing with heads high. The bodies are carved with feather pattern, with hollow bellies covered with feather wings. The incense is kept in the hollow bellies, and the fragrance floats out from the open mouths of the cranes. In the bottoms there are hill-stone-shaped copper lead base. Crane feet are tenoned with the base.

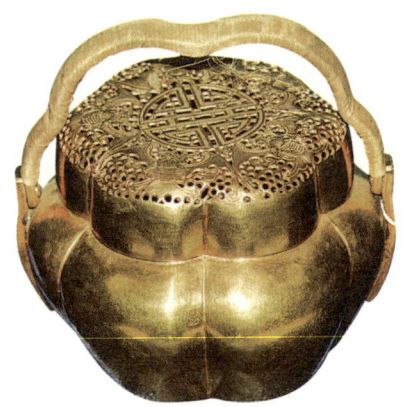

• 八成金手炉

手炉是古代宫廷乃至民间普遍使用的掌中取暖工具。明清时，手炉制作达到了高峰，成为达官贵族、富有人家的所用之物。其制作精致，造型多姿多彩，有圆形、方形、长方形、椭圆形、六角形、八角形、瓜棱形、梅花形、海棠形等。

Eighty Percentage Purity Gold Hand Warmer

Hand warmers were widely used from the court to folk in the hands for warming in ancient times. By the Ming and Qing dynasties, the hand warmers industry reached its peak and became the standard configuration among the nobles. The shapes are multiple, including round, square, rectangle, oblate, hexagon, octagon, melon-ridge shape, quincunx, cherry-apple shape and so on.

- 银烧蓝暖砚

严寒的冬季，古人会在砚盒内蓄以热水，使墨汁不冻，俗称"暖砚"。此砚盒呈长方形，盒上有盖，通体錾花鎏金，并嵌有烧蓝装饰，下有如意小足八个。底部錾有"大清乾隆年制"篆书款。砚盒通体錾刻浮雕式精美图案，由夔龙纹、云龙戏珠、缠枝花卉等纹饰组成，并镶嵌有烧蓝珐琅装饰。砚盒设计精巧，做工亦精细考究，外观显得极为华美，富丽堂皇。

Silver Burning Blue Warm Inkstone

In the cold winter, the ancients filled hot water in the inkstone to prevent the ink from freezing, which was called the Warm Inkstone. This inkstone is rectangle, having a cover on it. The body is designed with gilding and inlaid with Burning Blue decorations, with 8 *Ruyi*-shaped feet. A seal script inscription of "Made in Qianlong Period of the Qing Dynasty" is carved in the bottom face. The body is fully carved with beautiful pattern in relief style, which is composed with dragon, cloud dragons playing bead, branch and flower patterns and so on, and inset with burning blue enamel decorations. This inkstone is designed and crafted delicately, looking extremely luxuriant.

如意

如意是中国古人用以挠痒的器物，可如人意，因此得名。早期的如意长三尺（1米）左右，除用作挠痒外，还用作佛僧讲经指划所用。后来的如意长不过一二尺左右，专为玩赏、馈赠、进献和居室陈设之物。形状为长柄稍微弯曲，柄端呈灵芝或云头状，寓吉祥如意之意。明、清两代，如意与珍宝无异，俨然是一种吉祥、财富与权势的象征。尤其在清代，如意是宫中重要的陈设品，多置在宝座和寝室的几案上，供皇帝及嫔妃们玩赏。皇帝即位或生日时，大臣们常进献如意，一般为金或玉制。乾隆六十大寿时，皇宫大臣们自筹经费，专门制作了六十柄金丝编织的如意；慈禧六十岁生日时，大臣们进献了九九八十一柄如意。

Ruyi

Ruyi is a ware for scratching used by the ancient Chinese, the Chinese meaning of the name is "as one wishes". The *Ruyi* in the early time is about 3 *Chi* (1 meter) long, used to scratch or used by the monks for sermon. The subsequent one is about 1 to 2 *Chis* long specially used for playing with, gifting, offering tribute or the decorations in the house, shaped in long curly handle. The end is in lucid ganoderma or cloud shapes, which has an auspicious implied meaning. In the Ming and Qing dynasties, *Ruyi* became the major stuff in the palace, mostly placed on the tables beside the seats in the living rooms for the emperors and concubines to play with. When an emperor succeeded to the throne or on the birthday, the ministers usually presented *Ruyi* as a gift, which was mainly made of gold or jade. On Emperor Qianlong's 60th birthday, the ministers financed the fund by themselves and made 60 pieces of *Ruyi* weaved in gold wire. On Empress Dowager Cixi's 60th birthday, the ministers presented 81 pieces of *Ruyi*.

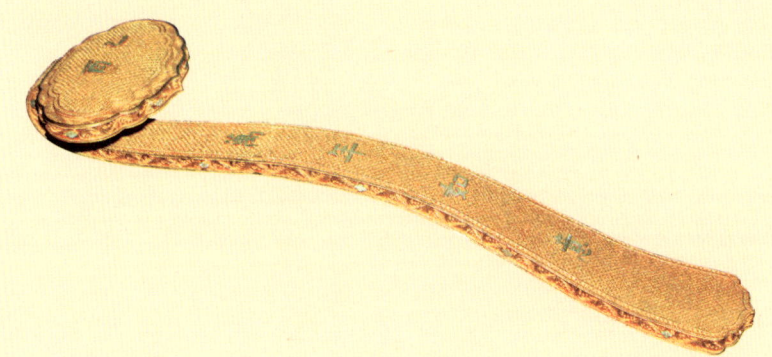

金累丝万年如意

此器为八成金质，采用累丝工艺，木胎。如意头的正面为累丝古钱纹，中心嵌绿松石"乙酉"二字；柄的正面亦为累丝古钱纹，镶嵌绿松石"萬年如意"四字；侧边以卷草纹为饰。此如意为一套六十柄之一，是乾隆皇帝六十寿辰时王公大臣们的进献之物，其做工精湛、细腻，是清代乾隆时期的典型作品。

Filigree Gold Eternity *Ruyi*

This article is made of gold with 80 percentage of purity, wood base with filigree. The front face is ancient coin pattern weaved of gold wire, inlaid with turquoise Chinese characters of *Yiyou* (a lunar year), and decorated by coiling grass design on the sides. The front side of the handle is also laced with ancient coin pattern and inset with the inscriptions of "*Ruyi* Forever"; the sides are decorated with curly grass pattern. This *Ruyi* is one of the 60s in a set, which were the tributes from the princes and ministers to Emperor Qianlong in his birthday of 60. The ware crafted delicately and smoothly, is a typical work of the Qianlong Period.

- **金錾花如意**

　此如意是用八成金錾花兼珠宝制作而成，如意头为嵌宝镂空花熏式样，在花熏内放上鲜花会散发芳香。

Gold *Ruyi* with Carved Patterns
This *Ruyi* is made of gold of 80 percentage purity with carved design and inlaid with gems. The head is a hollow censer container inlaid with gems, used for fresh flowers.

明清自鸣钟

　　明代万历年间，朝廷开始仿制西方的机械钟表。到了清代乾隆年间，乾隆皇帝对西方科学技术具有浓厚的兴趣，尤其喜爱欧洲的自鸣钟。当时除了大量进口欧洲精美、灵巧的钟表之外，还在宫内设自鸣钟处，保管、贮存及陈设自鸣钟。他在养心殿造办处增设了修理及制造自鸣钟的作坊，不但仿制出了具有逗人演技和悦耳音乐功能的机械钟表，还能制造出具有东方风格的钟表。

　　当时的自鸣钟主要供皇室观赏、宫廷陈设，所以大多精工细作，造型精美，并使用金、玉、漆、象牙、宝石、紫檀等贵重材质，使自鸣钟具有金碧辉煌的装饰效果。这些自鸣钟耗费了大量的人力物力，纯粹是皇宫贵族专享的奢侈品。嘉庆继位以后，由于嘉庆皇帝对西洋器物比较反感，自鸣钟处逐渐式微，制钟较少。

The Chime Clocks in the Ming and Qing Dynasties

During the Wanli Period of the Ming Dynasty, the court started to counterfeit the western mechanical clocks. By the Qianlong Period of the Qing Dynasty, the Emperor Qianlong showed rich interest in the western science and technology, especially the European chime clocks. Beside the massive imported European clocks, Qianlong set up the Chime Clock Department to save and display the chime clocks. He also established workshops to repair and make chime clocks in the Hall of Mental Cultivation Workshops, which not only counterfeited mechanical clocks with performing and music functions, but also made clocks in eastern style.

The chime clocks of that time were mainly used to be the decorations in the palace. Thus, most of them are in delicate crafts and beautiful shapes, and take precious materials including the gold, jade, painting, ivory, gem, rosewood and so on as raw materials, which display luxuriant decoration effect. The making of these chime clocks cost massive human power and materials purely for the luxurious enjoys of the royal court. Since the Emperor Jiaqing, the chime clock making was reduced gradually because he disliked western stuffs.

• 铜镀金珐琅升降塔钟
Gilding Copper Enamel Lift Tower Clock

● 铜镀金珐琅人物画自鸣钟
Gilding Copper Chime Clock with Enamel Figures

金银铤

　　金银铤，又称"金银锭"，是中国古代一种具有独特形制的金银币，呈束腰状。金银铤起源于南宋，造型优美，寓意吉祥，方便计数，利于储藏，是一种用于收藏贡奉的珍品。从唐代开始，金银铤就被用于朝廷储备和民间窖藏，甚至作为上贡、进奉的礼品，具有深厚的文化意蕴。

Gold and Silver Ingots

The gold and silver ingots, were kind of specially shaped gold and silver coins in ancient China, which are in waist-contract shape. The gold and silver ingots oriented in the Southern Song Dynasty (1127-1279), have beautiful shape and auspicious implied meanings. The gold and silver ingots are convenient for arithmetic and preservation, and are precious wares used as collection and tribute. Since the Tang Dynasty (618-907), the gold and silver ingots had been used by the court for preservation and by folk for saving, and even can be the tributes paid to the court, with deep cultural implication.

• 金铤
Gold Ingot

• 银铤
Silver Ingot